Date Due

WILLIAM BARCLAY:

a personal memoir

James Martin

WELCH PUBLISHING COMPANY INC.
Burlington, Ontario, Canada

First published in 1984 by
THE SAINT ANDREW PRESS
Edinburgh, Scotland

Second printing 1985

ISBN 0 920413 82 X

Copyright © 1984 James Martin

Welch Publishing Company Inc.
960 Gateway
Burlington, Ontario
L7L 5K7   Canada

Printed in Great Britain

CONTENTS

PREFACE

Few men have such a gift of communication as that enjoyed by William Barclay. In clear simple language he brought the Gospel message to life. The depth of his Christian convictions shone out of his writings like sunshine on a bright day. I never saw his name without my heart leaping upwards. He was an unfailing tonic for me.

Although I never had the joy of meeting William Barclay, I always looked on him as a friend. There must be many thousands who feel as I do about this man of God, and I rejoice that James Martin has written 'a personal memoir'.

It will be a treasure house for me.

London
August 1984

George Thomas
(Tonypandy)

INTRODUCTION

This book is for all those who met William Barclay, for all who would have liked to meet him and for all who have read any of his writings or heard any of his broadcasts. It is for William Barclay people.

Five years after his death I wrote an article for the Church of Scotland's magazine *Life and Work* which bore the title 'Remember Willie Barclay?' It evoked a flood of written response, revealing not only a widespread continuing remembrance of the man but also a deeply felt continuing affection.

That was enough to encourage me in the notion, which I held, of writing some kind of reminiscence of this great man beloved by so many; here it is.

I must stress that this book does not profess to be, and is not intended to be, a complete or exhaustive biography. Nor is it meant to be a critical appraisal of William Barclay's life and work. I was probably, in any case, too close to him and too fond of him to be fitted to write such a book.

This book is simply a recollection of William Barclay by one who was both a close friend and a great admirer. What I endeavour to do is to reflect some features of the man who, I believe, did more than anyone else in his generation to expound the New Testament and to advance the cause of its Saviour and Lord. I could have called it, I suppose, 'Faces of William Barclay', for it tries to recall him in different aspects. I hope that those readers who knew him personally may see here something of how they knew him best and that those readers who did not have that privilege may catch a glimpse of a truly great and lovable Christian scholar.

Whether or not Willie Barclay himself would have entirely approved of my treatment of him is a different question. He was fond of telling that story of how Oliver Cromwell repudiated a painting of him by a renowned artist of the day. Cromwell suffered from facial blemishes which the painter chose to ignore, producing instead an idealised portrait of the Protector. 'It won't do,' Cromwell thundered. 'Paint me as I am, warts and all.'

I fancy that would have been William Barclay's reaction, too, to an idealised portrait of himself. In fact he implied as much on one occasion. At the instigation of a publisher, I raised with him the possibility of my writing his biography while he was still on hand to supply detail and check facts. He refused. I recall him rasping, 'I'm not having any eulogy written about me while I'm still around to read it. Time enough when I'm dead.'

Willie Barclay had his warts—oh, yes. He was, for instance, suprisingly naïve in many respects. He was easily taken in, and sometimes people took advantage of his generous nature. He was argumentative and a coat-trailer (sometimes to the detriment of his reputation, as at times in his *Testament of Faith*). He could also be obstinate, and sometimes carelessly inaccurate in matters of fact.

But I am concerned in this book to deal with the attractive features, not the warts. My intention is to try to recall something of the glory that was William Barclay. What I have to write is unashamedly a panegyric but I hope and believe an honest and truthful one.

1: THE BARE BONES

William Barclay was born in Wick, in the north of Scotland, on 5 December 1907. He was the son, and only child, of a Gaelic-speaking bank manager from Fort William. This Highland bank manager was a devout Christian and a lay preacher; one, by his son's testimony, of no little ability.

Like all his friends, I frequently heard William Barclay speak with affection and with gratitude of his parents. Time and again he would express patently sincere thanks for the good fortune he had enjoyed in having such a fine father and mother. He used to speak often of his parents and many a time would refer to how his mother died a very painful death through cancer of the spine. Such a reference was mostly in conjunction with a quiet but vehement declaration that the God of Love revealed in Jesus Christ most certainly would not wish or decree an individual's suffering and pain.

William Barclay was only 24 years of age when his mother died, and due shortly to leave divinity college and be licensed as a preacher of the Gospel. Often in later years he would tell how his father then, himself grief-stricken, said to him, 'You'll have a new note in your preaching now.'

In his book *Testament of Faith*, in which he quotes this very occasion, William Barclay goes on to say, 'The last thing she ever gave me was a soft leather sermon case; from that day to this, more than 40 years later, I never went into a pulpit without it. I thank God on every remembrance of my mother.'

The Barclays moved from Wick to Motherwell in 1912, when William's father was transferred to his Bank's branch in that town. This was a formative period in William Barclay's life and one on which he always looked back with much happiness and gratitude. Although born in Wick, he regarded himself as a Motherwell man. Since I was born and brought up in that town, this became a strong bond of connection between us.

His secondary schooling took place at Dalziel High School and his was a distinguished sojourn there. When, years later, I too became a pupil at that same school, I used to see his name in gilt lettering on more than one of the honour boards on display in the assembly hall. He became Captain of the school, *Dux* of the school, Athletics Champion and much more, displaying already in his boyhood and very early manhood that versatility of talent which was to be one of the hallmarks of his later life.

All the rest of his life he looked back with joy and pride on the years he spent at Dalziel. It may well be, as it is with most of us, that William Barclay's memory of past days tended to be selective, highlighting the good and overlooking the not so good. Nevertheless, his recollections of Dalziel seemed to be of total joy and were attended with much gratitude. To the end of his days he was one who never failed to be humbly and sincerely grateful for any benefit or service received, whoever the giver might be. He considered his debt to Dalziel High School a large one and often thanked God for it.

It was at Dalziel that the love of games he had acquired from his father found development and scope; he had a natural aptitude and he became proficient at a number of different sports. Here, too, that love of music which characterised all his later life, and which was probably his mother's gift, blossomed and thrived. He was always particularly grateful for the fact that Dalziel High inculcated in him that love for the Greek language which was, of course, central to the work of expounding the New Testament, which he was to perform so magnificently in later years.

On leaving school, he went to Glasgow University. First of all he entered the Faculty of Arts, emerging in due time with his Master of Arts degree and a first-class honours in Classics. He then went on to Trinity College, Glasgow, to undergo training for the ministry of the Church and take the degree of Bachelor of Divinity (with distinction in New Testament). Characteristically, he used often to speak affectionately and with gratitude of the teachers he sat under there and of the immense debt in which their learning, their teaching, but most of all their personalities, had placed him.

William Barclay not only gained much from his time at Trinity College in terms of knowledge and inspiration; he also, less predictably, gained himself a wife and for this, too, he was ever grateful. The divinity students had lunch together ('common dinner') in the college and one of the cooks in Barclay's time was a certain Katherine Gillespie, a daughter of the manse, whose father exercised a ministry of more than 40 years' duration in the Ayrshire parish of Dundonald. When the time came for William Barclay to depart from the college, it had been decided that the cook would be his bride and they married in June 1933.

After his BD graduation in 1932 he spent a year of further study in Germany at Marburg University. At the end of that year he was ordained and inducted to the pastoral charge of Trinity Church, Renfrew. This, as it turned out, was to be not just his first but also his only pastoral charge.

He continued as minister of Trinity Church, Renfrew, until the end of 1946, and at the beginning of 1947 he took up the post of Lecturer in New Testament Language and Literature at his *alma mater*, the University of Glasgow. Later, he was promoted to Senior Lecturer and later still, on the retirement of the Professor, the man he was always pleased to call his 'chief', G H C Macgregor, William Barclay was appointed to the Chair and so became, in 1964, Professor of Divinity and Biblical Criticism, a position which he held until his retirement in September 1974.

In 1956 the University of Edinburgh conferred on him the honorary degree of Doctor of Divinity; in 1969 he was made a Commander of the British Empire (CBE) in the Queen's New Year Honours list. His retirement from his professorial Chair saw him accept an offer from Collins Publishers, through his good friend of many years, Ian Chapman, to provide him with an office and a secretary, so that he could continue his writing. Three years later, on reaching his seventieth birthday, he retired also from this working routine; the following month, on 24 January 1978, he died.

2: THE MINISTER

William Barclay's call to be minister of Trinity Church, Renfrew, came to him in the middle of 1933; and his ordination and induction duly took place shortly afterwards. This process occupied no more than the usual few weeks, but in a very real sense the process that culminated in his installation as parish minister in Renfrew had begun a long way back. No doubt the process began in his early boyhood, but probably was more directly related to an experience which befell him on a hillside overlooking Fort William in the north of Scotland.

His father had been preaching at the evening service in the local church and his sermon had been well received. After the service, father and son walked home together. It was then, according to his own testimony, that the young William decided for the ministry. It was sudden and it was sure; it was vivid and it was dramatic. As Willie told the story himself (which he did on numerous occasions) he was walking along the road, thinking about his father's preaching, when all at once he found his mind saying, 'That's what I want to do with my life. What the old man can do, I can do, too.' He used to say that ever afterwards he could even identify the very stone in the road that he was gazing at when the revelation struck him; when the call was heard and the response made.

However his decision was arrived at, it was certainly clear; it was also firm and it was to prove enduring. The plough to which William Barclay resolved to put his hand that night, he followed the rest of his life.

It was in October 1925 that he enrolled at the University of Glasgow and began the studies which led to his graduation as Master of Arts (Hons) in the summer of 1929. It happened, therefore, that his entry upon his Divinity Course at Trinity College, Glasgow, in the autumn of that same year coincided with the culmination of the great events that brought together the Church of Scotland and the United Free Church of Scotland in an Act of Union in the very same month.

William Barclay had been brought up in the United Free Church and it was to the United Free Church College that he went to be trained as a minister. But Trinity College was now training men for the ministry of the reunited Church of Scotland, so when he attained his Bachelor of Divinity degree with distinction, he was licensed to preach the Gospel as a Licentiate of the Church of Scotland.

There was no one, perhaps, in whom the old denominational prejudices were less likely to linger than in William Barclay. At the same time his roots in the United Free Church had been well established and his experiences there both happy and enriching. It may, therefore, have been more than mere coincidence that the call to his first parish should come from a church which had come into the Union from the United Free side.

The 14 years he spent as minister in Trinity Church, Renfrew, were very happy ones for him. That church and its people had a special place in his heart to the day he died. No doubt in this instance, as I suggested may well have been the case regarding his schooldays, and as is the perhaps fortunate case with most of us in many instances, his memory was somewhat selective, tending to recall vividly the sunshine and to forget the gloom. One might have thought, listening to him reminiscing about his Renfrew days, that never a cloud darkened the congregational sky and that somehow Willie B was spared entirely the rubs, disappointments and heartaches that every other parish minister seems to experience to a greater or lesser degree.

The fact is, of course, that William Barclay, too, had his share of discouragement and frustration in the exercise of his parish ministry. It is also a fact, however, that his ministry in Renfrew was attended by much joy and blessing. No further confirmation of this is needed other than to say that, just as Barclay remembered Renfrew and his years there with grateful affection, so do Renfrew and its people remember his ministry there with gratitude and love, even though it was as long ago as 1947 that William Barclay moved from Trinity Church.

The secret was that the William Barclay who went to Renfrew as a young minister was basically the same person who, in later years, became an internationally acclaimed New Testament expositor. Similarly, many of the foundations of the fame and success of the later Barclay were laid, or at least made secure, during those Renfrew years. Here he learned much of his trade; patterns were set for the future and keys, that were to open many doors still to come his way, were cast.

Not least was this true of his supreme ability to communicate which was to do so much for the cause of Christ and at the same time make William Barclay an international household name.

One day, in the course of an afternoon's visiting, he called on an elderly female member of the congregation. After they had been chatting for a time, she suddenly said to her young minister, 'I'm just wondering to myself why it is that when you are speaking to me here at my own fireside, I can understand easily everything you say, and yet sometimes when you are in the pulpit, I can't follow you at all.'

That remark made a deep impression on the young William Barclay, and he went home to think very seriously about its implications. Out of that came a resolve to do everything he could to ensure that, whenever he spoke in public, he would employ language that everyone in his audience could readily understand. This resolve, from which he never recanted, was one of the foundations on which his future enormous success as a communicator came to be built.

In Renfrew, too, his avid interest in people was immediately in evidence. William Barclay was always a good mixer and he certainly mixed well in Renfrew. He was instantly at home and on good terms with all the different age groups and kinds of people he found in his congregation and in the town. In particular he quickly established a rapport with the youth of the area. This was perhaps a precursor of the vast volume of writing he was later to produce specifically for the benefit of young people.

It was while he was minister of Trinity Church, Renfrew, that he began his illustrious career as a writer and expositor. Here he began to write regularly for the Sunday School Union's monthly magazine for teachers, providing Bible reading notes for their guidance. Soon, in addition, he was being asked by the Church of Scotland's Youth Committee to write Bible Class handbooks and by the Executive of the Boys' Brigade to perform a similar service on their behalf.

First and foremost, however, he carried out conscientiously his duties as minister of Trinity Church. He worked hard at the usual round of Sunday services and weekday meetings, organisations and committees, visitations to homes and hospitals, along with the tasks of baptising, marrying and burying. Although these might be considered routine, Barclay always treated each one as special.

During these years he also became a family man, with the birth first of a son, Ronald, and then of a daughter, Barbara. As with most parish ministers, because their work requires them to be 'out on the job' nearly every night of the week, winter and summer, William Barclay rarely spent as much time with his wife and family as either they or he would have wished. He accepted it, however, as one of the sacrifices that had to be made and despite it the Barclays managed to have and to maintain a warm family relationship.

Barclay in those Renfrew days, addicted to hard work though he was, also managed to ensure that there were regular leisure periods in his weekly schedule. From his earliest days he had had a passion for sport, a passion which remained with him to the end. This passion he was able to indulge both as an active participant and as a spectator while he was minister of Trinity Church.

Soccer was always his favourite sport; he had been a valuable member of the Dalziel High School Senior XI. He played no competitive football after he left school, although he did on occasion turn out in charity matches. It is a matter of fond personal reminiscence that, on his last appearance in a football jersey, I played on the same side.

This was in the annual Clergy versus Police match at Govan in Glasgow, one of the events in the ancient yearly local festival known as the Govan Fair. The Clergy team was a mixture of Protestant ministers and Roman Catholic priests. Barclay played at left back that night, I played at centre forward and the result was a draw; three goals each.

Although he played little soccer after his induction to Trinity Church, Renfrew, William Barclay spectated a great deal. He was, and remained, an ardent follower of what he counted his home-town team, Motherwell, and regularly went to see them play. As time went by, he introduced first Ronnie and then Barbara to the same pursuit.

While he played little football after he became a minister, he continued to play a fair amount of golf. He was one of those natural ball players with a good eye who become at least reasonably proficient at any game they take up. He played a good game of golf and for many years had a single figure handicap.

In Renfrew, however, as in later years, work was his main passion; just as he established or developed here many of the 'basics' of his later and wider ministry, so he established or developed many of those convictions about the parish ministry which he held so strongly and was never afraid to express.

These convictions he sometimes put down in print, but often expounded in private conversations.

The reason was that they were important to him, just as the parish ministry was. The major portion of his working life came to be spent on the staff of a university but he never deviated from his opinion that the parish ministry was the most important task any man could ever undertake for God. It was in fact because he saw his university job as a help to the making of better parish ministers that he agreed to enter that sphere.

Here are six principles he believed to be vital for the proper discharge of the parish ministry.

1 The ministry is, and must always be, a full-time job.

The minister, in his opinion, was minister of his congregation and parish all the time, every hour of every day, unless he was physically absent, say on holiday, from his parish. He had to be available at all times, for no one could possibly legislate when the moment of dire and urgent need might arise in the life of someone in the congregation.

He used to tell of the minister—and indeed wrote of him in his *Testament of Faith* (p 7)—who took issue with him on this viewpoint and insisted that *he* had educated his people not to ask him to do anything on a Monday. Barclay commented scathingly: 'I suppose he must have had an arrangement with God that no one in his congregation died on a Monday, that no home was stricken with some tragedy, that no one needed God. There are some things which will not wait; if they are not done now, they cannot be done at all.'

2 The minister's first priority should always be his ministry and its obligations.

Barclay took a poor view of those who allowed other things—a church committee, perhaps, or some other extra-parochial interest—to have the prior claim. 'To put it at its lowest level,' he would bark, 'the minister ought to do first and foremost the job for which he is being paid.'

3 The minister should put the time he has available to the best possible use.

While he believed in the importance of regular time off, he was deeply concerned at what he reckoned was a quite appalling wasting of time on the part of most ministers. 'So many people,' he would say, 'think that ten minutes is only a period of time to kill. They think it is far too short a period in which to do anything really worthwhile; but if every minister would discipline himself to make the best possible use of every "spare" ten minutes, what a difference it would make.'

There was never any better example than himself of the practice he was advocating here. He regarded time as God's gift and he tried always to employ it in the consciousness that this was so.

4 The minister must be a good mixer and relate well to all kinds of people.

William Barclay had little time for the minister who wanted to live in some remote ivory tower, largely detached from the day-to-day lives of his congregation. Although he recognised that some men are naturally more gregarious than others, he nevertheless felt strongly that every minister worth his salt should be sufficiently interested in his people to be able to get alongside them in their work and play, in their hopes and fears, in their successes and failures, in their joys and sorrows.

5 Preaching is one of the most vital aspects of the ministry.

William Barclay subscribed not at all to the tendency to play down the role of preaching. For him the preaching of the Gospel of Jesus Christ from pulpit or platform was supremely important.

It was one of Barclay's great regrets that he could never give the Warrack Lectures on the subject of Preaching, to which fuller reference is made in the next chapter. Nevertheless, he did manage to pass on many extremely valuable and helpful observations on the subject through his writing, his public speaking and in private conversation and discussion with friends. He believed that certain rules ought to apply to preaching, and these were:

a) A man should be in the job of preaching only if he had something to say that had to be said. If he were to occupy a pulpit and preach sermons week by week and year by year, then it ought to be because he had good news, which could not be kept to himself, to proclaim.

b) The message should be sincere; it ought to be the preacher's own testimony. Not in the sense of being completely original. Not in the sense of drawing nothing from anyone else's learning or experience. But in the sense of being something he himself knew to be true. Nothing, Barclay was fond of repeating, ever showed up so plainly in a preacher as insincerity or lack of conviction. Unless the preacher had a passionate belief in what he was saying, his hearers were likely to meet it with at best indifference and at worst derision.

c) A sermon should contain some element of teaching. He was inclined to look with a wary eye on the preacher who insisted on being 'topical' every Sunday; who, as he put it, seemed to look more in the direction of the newspapers than the Bible for his text. It was not that he considered sermons should take no account of what was currently happening in the world; far from it. He was always himself alive to current affairs and his awareness of them was frequently reflected in the sermons he preached. But he looked very much askance at the preacher who seemed to think that topicality was everything and appeared to be in danger of forgetting the necessity to anchor his message in the Bible.

Here is how he once expressed this conviction: 'Preaching ought to be biblically and credally centred. This is far from saying that preaching should never deal with the social, political and economic situation, but it is to say that it should start from the Christian book and the Christian belief' (*Testament of Faith*, p 79).

6 The importance of pastoral visitation cannot be over-emphasised.

Many might be surprised to learn that William Barclay wrote: 'Early on in my ministry, and in some ways even to the end of it, I dreaded pastoral visitation' (*Testament of Faith*, p 69). He confessed that he found it 'the most difficult and exhausting' part of his work as a parish minister, but that did not mean that he avoided it.

Only those who knew him really well came to realise that he was possessed of an innate shyness that made knocking on doors and initiating conversations matters of real effort, and often of some torment. Those of us who have experienced something of the same agony appreciate all the more the high quality of William Barclay's pastoral ministry in Renfrew as evidenced by the affection towards him which he inspired among his people there. This was because he went among them in their homes as a warm-hearted, compassionate friend who was at the same time an emissary of the Lord Jesus Christ.

William Barclay left Trinity Church, Renfrew, in December 1947 and never held another pastoral charge. But till the day he died he never ceased to be first and foremost a minister of the Gospel. This was not just in name, although of course he retained in full, all his days, the status of a minister of the Church. Despite the fact that he no longer had a pastoral tie with a congregation, he continued to exercise a very active and valuable ministry. Until the last few years of his life he used to preach most Sundays, often away from home, as well as address-ing evening meetings through the week. Even more, he continued to exercise a pastoral ministry, especially after he became famous, through his un-flagging industry and inexhaustible compassion in responding to the unceasing flow of letters, tele-phone calls and personal visits which poured in upon him. He never seemed to grow tired of these things, and he certainly never betrayed any an-noyance or exasperation because of them.

It is little wonder that the people of Renfrew and of Trinity Church in particular remember with great pride and thanks William Barclay and the years he spent among them.

3: THE PREACHER

William Barclay was dedicated to preaching; and a magnificent preacher he was. He would have been quick to repudiate that description and would have done so not for reasons of false modesty but out of sincere conviction. He never counted himself an outstanding preacher; and yet he surely was.

He was not, it is true, a preacher in the romantic mould. Not for him the purple passages and the frequent dramatic climaxes that once were the mark of Scottish pulpit oratory at its best. What is more, he had a rasping kind of voice which was once described as sounding like two bricks being rubbed vigorously together. This was coupled with a broad Lanarkshire accent which never forsook him.

One of his beloved teachers at Trinity College, Glasgow, was A B McAulay of whom he never failed to speak with respect and even awe. He used to tell with considerable relish how McAulay said to him once during his student days, 'Barclay, if you don't get rid of that accent, you'll never get anywhere in the Church.'

His accent, however, did not change, nor did the abrasive quality of his voice suffer any refinement as the years passed. Nevertheless, he was, in the opinion of many, a prince of preachers. If the chief end of preaching is—as must surely be generally agreed—the communication of Gospel truth, then William Barclay fulfilled that purpose to a degree that was perhaps unequalled by any of his contemporaries and certainly not, I think, surpassed.

It was a matter of disappointment, both to himself and his friends, that William Barclay could not be chosen to give the Warrack Lectures on Preaching. The Warrack Lectureship was founded to promote the art of preaching; and its intention was that someone who had proved himself to be an effective and attractive preacher should be invited to deliver a series of lectures on the subject to students in training for the ministry.

A prohibition written into the Trust Deed stipulated that no one could be appointed who occupied a position in any of the four Scottish divinity colleges. This meant that, as soon as he became first Lecturer, and then Professor, in the New Testament Department at Trinity College, William Barclay was automatically debarred from ever delivering these lectures. He said to me on several occasions, more than a little wistfully, that one of his ambitions, now never to be fulfilled, had been to be chosen for the Warrack Lectureship because, as he put it, he felt he had learned a few things about preaching that he would have liked to pass on.

Barclay always maintained that preaching, to be worthy of the name, should have something important to say and should say it clearly and convincingly. I was privileged to see and hear him many times at work in the pulpit and I never ceased to marvel at the seemingly effortless fashion in which, with unfailing regularity, he captivated his audience and presented his message to them in such lucid and compelling terms.

It is a rather odd circumstance then that, despite his immense popularity as a preacher and what seemed to all others his undoubted success in the pulpit, Barclay himself did not have a very high estimate of his preaching ability.

It has been said that there is never any true preaching 'without the shedding of blood'. From my own acquaintance with him I know that William Barclay's preaching was something that he found very demanding. This statement might well sound strange to many who saw and heard him preach with apparently effortless ease. The fact is, however, that preaching was something that he regarded so highly and took so seriously that he was never able to preach except at considerable personal cost. One consequence of this was that, in his later years when he had become less vigorous physically, he found preaching an increasingly demanding and exhausting burden and could be persuaded to take it up only on special and progressively less frequent occasions.

That, however, was only in his last few years. Previously, as I have said, nearly every Sunday found him in a pulpit. He was generous to a fault with his time and energy, and found it difficult to refuse any request that his diary informed him he could accommodate, even if it meant considerable inconvenience to him personally.

It became, therefore, practically impossible to have William Barclay as a guest preacher anywhere unless the arrangements were made long in advance; his diary filled up so quickly. This makes understandable, to some extent at least, the telephone call that came to him one evening when I was with him in his study. When the call was completed, he remarked to me, 'That was so-and-so (naming a former student of his) asking me if I would baptise their baby.' 'Oh,' I said, 'I hadn't heard that they'd had a child.' 'They haven't yet,' said Willie. 'The baby's not due for another seven months.'

That William Barclay found it difficult to say 'no' to any request for his services is a fact to which his overcrowded diary bore constant witness. This applied to week-night speaking engagements as much as to Sunday worship. In the case of the former his range of topics and the variety of the occasions demonstrated a remarkable versatility. He was just as likely, on any given night, to be guest speaker at the annual dinner of Motherwell Cricket Club or the Renfrew Philatelic Society as giving the address at a Sunday School Parents' Night or Church Anniversary.

He could and did speak not only with fluency but also out of a wealth of knowledge on a number of subjects. His interests were many and varied, embracing such diverse things as stamp-collecting, trains and sport. He was an excellent speaker on Robert Burns and gave the Immortal Memory at as many Burns' Suppers as could be fitted into his programme. His first speaking love was, however, also his most enduring. He found his greatest satisfaction in expounding some aspect of his beloved Gospel, whether from pulpit or from platform.

All his public utterances were marked by a thorough knowledge of the subject in hand and invariably accompanied by a wealth of background detail and a mass of illustrative material, all of which combined to make a very vivid presentation.

I well remember the first time I heard him speak. I was still at school but a Sunday School teacher, and as such attended the annual 'At Home' of the Motherwell Sunday School Union. William Barclay was the speaker. In the course of his address he used an anecdote about a preacher telling a story of a man caught in a storm at sea and telling it so realistically that a listener in the gallery suddenly called out excitedly, 'He's overboard!' Barclay himself had a quite remarkable ability to make things vividly real in his speaking and I for one never knew him to be dull. Like G K Chesterton he counted it the worst of sins 'to call a green leaf grey'.

In addition, he was far and away the best ever I encountered at the discussion sessions which frequently followed his speaking at one of the less formal meetings he took such delight in addressing. His strength here derived from four sources.

First was his meticulous preparation beforehand. His style was deceptively relaxed, even casual, but in fact he never stood up to give any sort of address anywhere without this. No matter what the occasion, be it a church service in some large building packed to capacity or a tiny meeting in a small back hall, he always did his homework assiduously. He came to every occasion knowing exactly what he was going to say and how he was going to say it. In addition, he had steeped himself so thoroughly in his subject that, whatever questions might be asked and whatever corner of the field might come to be explored, he was in total command.

Second was his marvellous ability to get to the heart of a questioner's question. I have never known

anyone match his faculty for grasping questions
from the body of the hall. He was able often to see
the question lying behind some not very well
chosen words much more clearly than the questioner saw it himself.

Third was the way in which he dealt with every
question as if it were the most important and the
most fascinating he had ever been asked.

Fourth was his probably unrivalled ability
(characteristic of all his speaking and writing) to
express himself in simple, clear terms that anyone
and everyone could understand. Following that resolve made in the early days of his Renfrew ministry, he always spoke in terms that were readily
intelligible to his audience whatever its nature or
size, and never chose a multi-syllabic word when a
single syllable would convey his meaning just as
accurately. That was why it could be said of
William Barclay, truthfully and with no hint of
blasphemy, 'The common people heard him
gladly'.

4: THE UNIVERSITY TEACHER

The mere statistics of William Barclay's university teaching career—appointed Lecturer 1947, appointed Professor 1963, retired 1974—do not by themselves give any indication of the giant of a man he became in his teaching life. But giant of a man he was, in the opinion of the mass of his students at least, and in the last resort whose opinion matters more than theirs?

I was never a student of his but I knew, and know, many who were. Not all of them adored him; a few disliked his theology and his biblical standpoint too intensely for that, but the majority did.

No one, I think, would seriously claim that William Barclay added many new insights or opened up many new avenues in the realm of New Testament scholarship. He himself used to say that he never had an original idea in his life, but was a theological 'middleman' who simply peddled in down-to-earth language the ideas and findings of other scholars.

This was the sort of characteristically self-deprecating remark that he used at times to throw into conversation, a remark that he more than half believed himself but which is patently at odds with the facts of the case. The fact is that he was a brilliant scholar and quite often an original one. Nevertheless it is true that he did not contribute much in the way of fresh discovery to the field of biblical scholarship. That was neither his forte nor his avowed intent.

His aim was to distil the best of existing knowledge and to present it to his students in the most attractive and intelligible way that he could. In the fulfilment of that aim he was without peer. Class after class of students would testify to that. He excited them, he informed them and, perhaps above all, he stimulated their interest in the New Testament and what it had to say.

It had been a real wrench for him to leave his pastoral charge at Renfrew, for he loved his work there and his people. He had, however, little hesitation in accepting the invitation when it came. Truly humble though he was, he believed that he could and would make a good teacher and was eager to undertake a job which, he realised, would give him the opportunity of influencing and shaping the ministers of the future.

He was a success from the outset. Professor Garth Macgregor, I know, found him an ideal assistant. Student after student has written to me, on learning that I was endeavouring to write this book, saying how highly they regarded William Barclay as a teacher. And this in most cases was not simply because of the mass of information he conveyed to them so lucidly and in such easily digestible form on the given subject, but even more because of the way in which his enthusiasm for the New Testament had infected and enthused them.

One writes to me: 'I recall again and again coming out of NT with a glow in the heart, feeling after Willie's lecture what a grand thing it was to be a Christian, one's knowledge increased and enthusiasm kindled.'

The tremendously high regard in which he was

held by most of the students who passed through his hands was not only because of the quality of his teaching, but also, and perhaps even more, because of his interest in and concern for the students as individuals. Pastoral ministry was not something he left behind when he departed from Renfrew; he simply diverted its flow into a different channel.

The same former student whom I quoted earlier said also, 'I recall first and foremost a great human being who knew all the lads by their Christian names and was genuinely interested in them.' He would sit with the students at coffee break, enquire about them and their families, and encourage them to seek him out to discuss problems large and small. Many ministers scattered far and wide throughout the world today thank God for the Christian compassion shown them and the active help given them by their Professor Barclay.

Students of his, while they were at college, and ever afterwards too, had a special place in his affections and were always special objects of assistance if ever assistance was needed. This was so even if the said object proved himself quite lacking in grace or gratitude, as was the case in one sad and notorious instance.

A former student of Willie's had got himself into a very deep morass of debt and in addition serious charges of fraud were pending. The man in question was meanwhile admitted to a psychiatric ward in one of our Scottish hospitals some distance from Glasgow. From there he sent a message to his former Professor, begging for help. For some weeks William Barclay, despite his many other commitments and his always busy schedule, drove up and down the road between his home and that hospital so that his former student would have a regular visitor. In addition he gave him a loan to enable him to pay off his debts, in the hope of averting prosecution.

The man in question was eventually discharged from hospital. His court case was still pending and he lost little time in fleeing the country. Willie Barclay was much hurt by the whole affair, not so much because the minister made no attempt to repay any of the money loaned but chiefly because 'he never even said thank you'.

There was a sequel to this true tale. One night, much later, I received a telephone call from Glasgow's Barlinnie prison. It was a detective officer who also happened to be one of my elders. 'I have just arrested Revd ——— on his return to this country from abroad. He would like you to contact Professor Barclay and ask him to come and see him.' I passed on the message and, despite the hurt and disappointment of his previous experience, Willie visited his former student in prison and helped him once again, acting just as he believed his Lord would have wanted him to do.

No student of William Barclay's needed to have any hesitation in approaching him, whether it was for simple conversation, seeking information, or asking for advice or assistance. Many were the Barclay students, both while at college and in later years, who did approach him for one or more of such reasons. No one was ever refused and no one ever went away without being helped in some way.

Part of the reason for the high regard in which his

students held him was his consideration and compassion for them even when they occupied theological and biblical standpoints that differed from his. I had a letter from a former student of his in which he told me that, since he had been brought up in a strongly evangelical tradition, he 'commenced the New Testament class in no little fear and trepidation, for was it not true that the Professor would cut one's faith to shreds? It was *not* true—he was a marvellous teacher, wonderfully patient and kind.'

Every student mattered to him as an individual person. That was the secret. The same former student I have just quoted also had this reminiscence of his first college year.

'On the very first day the roll was called, but that was it, and we really did not think that Professor Barclay had a clue as to who any of us were. I was doing an attachment and because of the illness of the minister, I preached much more often in the first couple of months than the regulations permitted.

'One day I was descending the college stairs when I heard my name called and turned to see Professor Barclay's finger beckoning me to his side. Terrified, I went back up the stairs and faced the great man.

"You are a student in ———— Church?"

"Yes, sir." (How does *he* know?)

"The minister's not keeping too well?"

"No, sir." (Goodness, he knows that, too.)

"You're being made to work pretty hard, I know. See that you don't overdo it and, remember, if ever you need any help or advice, I am always here."'

Another characteristic of Barclay the university teacher which added to his students' respect for him, and at the same time demonstrated further his concern for them and their training for the ministry, was his pre-lecture prayer. It was a long-established custom that every lecture in every subject was prefaced by a short prayer led by the lecturer. In William Barclay's case, this prayer was never allowed to become a mere matter of form. It would have been only too easy for it to become a very perfunctory affair, and perhaps even the same combination of words mouthed lecture after lecture and year after year. Barclay's pre-lecture prayers, on the other hand, became legendary. They were both a model and an inspiration. Prepared with exceeding thoroughness in advance and typed out on small cards, in a few short sentences they covered a wide range of relevant subjects and evoked much ready response in many student hearts. In particular they appreciated his Friday prayers, for they invariably contained an intercession for all who would be helping to lead church worship on the coming Sunday.

It was no surprise to those who knew him that William Barclay did not hesitate to let some of his prodigious energy be employed outside the walls of his lecture room. He played a very full part, and a most valuable one, for instance, in the administrative side of Trinity College and the Faculty of Divinity: but perhaps the two extramural activities most worth mentioning are his involvement in the American Summer School of Theology and his conductorship of the Trinity College Choir.

The American School of Theology was very much a William Barclay brainchild and he was very fond of his offspring. In co-operation with Revd Bob Martin of Princeton, USA, another former

Barclay student, he devised, organised and largely motivated a School of Theology for American ministers and friends that took place in Scotland at St Andrews every July for a number of years. I was privileged to take part in the programme on a couple of occasions and I can testify that the whole affair was both very popular and very enjoyable. Many American pastors and their families remember these occasions with great gladness.

Strictly speaking Willie Barclay did not originate the Trinity College Choir. There had been one in former years. But he it was who revived it after he joined the teaching staff, and for many years, indeed until his retirement from his Chair, he presided over its activities and conducted its singing. The choir rehearsed every Friday afternoon during term and usually gave five concerts a year; four on Friday evenings in selected churches (and there were always far more seeking to have the choir than could be accommodated) and the final one in the college itself for relatives and friends. In addition, the choir and its conductor did a week's tour during the Easter vacation when a Presbytery was visited, concerts were given, the students preached in various churches on the Sunday and the call to the ministry was sounded out loud and clear in that region. The Trinity College Choir rehearsals, concerts and tours were great fun and were also, in their own distinctive fashion, a witness to the faith which was the common bond linking all the participants together. One of the most abiding memories of what were always light-hearted occasions was the way in which the Professor each year carefully honed two jokes and used them in his introductory remarks at every concert, and another was the way in which at the outset he would give to every church audience the freedom to applaud as much as they liked 'because you are perfectly safe. We don't know any encores.'

William Barclay was an extremely popular university teacher. He was also a very able one. It was, therefore, a considerable surprise to many when he announced his intention of retiring when he did, still a few years short of the age of seventy when retirement would have been compulsory. He seemed still so full of energy, but when someone put the question to him, 'Why don't you carry on a bit longer?', he replied, 'It's a wise man who knows when to let down the barrow.'

5: THE WRITER

William Barclay performed a magnificent work with his pen for Christ and his kingdom.

It started back in his Renfrew days when he began writing material for the Sunday School Union. Many of his books written originally for a particular readership have since been revised by me on the author's behalf and republished with a more general readership in mind. These include, for instance, *The King and the Kingdom, And Jesus Said, Ambassador for Christ, The Old Law and the New Law* and *And He Had Compassion.*

For many years Barclay was never able to tell precisely how many books of his had been published. Even now it is difficult, if not impossible, to arrive at an exact reckoning, for some of his writings are not at all easy to categorise. It would appear, however, that he wrote somewhere in the region of 70 books. (A full list is given on pp 99–104.)

In his prime, and his writing prime extended until the last year or two of his life, William Barclay's output was prodigious. Once, when someone commented on his unusual absence from the Students' Common Room during the 45 minute mid-morning break between lectures, a fellow-professor remarked, 'He's probably just stayed in his room to write another book.'

He wrote at great speed. This was made possible by the manner in which he always made sure that it was all in his head and in his heart before he put pen to paper (or fingers to typewriter, to be more precise). Another Barclay writing characteristic was that he hardly ever took time to revise what he had written and never took time to polish it up.

I vividly remember one day in the earlier years of our friendship calling upon him in his room at the university. He was busily engaged tapping away at his typewriter. 'Just give me a moment,' he said, 'till I finish this article. It has to go off today.' He typed on rapidly for a few minutes more; then he extracted the paper from the machine, folded it, placed it in the already addressed envelope beside him, sealed the envelope and turned to speak to me. 'Aren't you going to read it over?' I asked in some horror. 'Don't let my being here keep you from doing so.' 'Oh,' he replied, 'it has nothing to do with your being here. I never spend time reading over anything I have written. It would waste too much time.' As I got to know him better, I came to realise that this was exactly and invariably his way.

This method of his had definite drawbacks, as I found out only too well when I accepted the task of revising for its new edition the 17 commentary volumes of his Daily Study Bible series. But I have no doubt that this was the correct method for him. He was so anxious to get on with his task of communicating the Good News in print that he was simply not prepared to have precious time taken up with what in his opinion was a comparatively unimportant process of literary embellishment. Had he taken time to do the polishing of his work that most writers consider essential, the world might well have been several Barclay books the poorer; what a loss that would have been.

William Barclay's ruling and passionate concern in his writing was to make the New Testament message clear and persuasive and he achieved this objective in quite marvellous fashion. As a result many thousands throughout the world owe a great deal to his gift of communication and his dedicated use of it.

I can think personally of many who belong to this category and I know of many more. I think, for instance, of a certain young woman, a new communicant member of my congregation, who had been admitted to hospital for what turned out to be a very lengthy stay. On one of my visits to her I gave her a copy of William Barclay's Daily Study Bible commentary on the Gospel of St Matthew. On my very next visit, she greeted me with a radiant face and simply could not thank me enough for my gift.

'Mr Martin,' she said, 'ever since I took my church membership vows, I have read a portion of St Matthew's Gospel every day, but it is only since you gave me that book of William Barclay's that I have begun to understand it properly; and it has made such a wonderful difference to me.'

There are so many true stories of the help given to so many people by the Barclay books. Here are another three.

A friend of mine who had emigrated to the United States said to me once on a visit back home, 'We have an active Bible Study group in our [Presbyterian] church over in the States and we regularly use the Barclay commentaries as our basis of study. One of the most enthusiastic members of our group is a Roman Catholic lady. She came along one night and asked if she might be allowed to join us. The reason for her request, she told us, was that she had heard we used William Barclay's books and she owed her Christian faith to reading one of them.'

One day an engineer came to the home of an elderly house-bound lady to repair her refrigerator. In the course of his visit the lady, who had been a regular churchgoer, asked him, 'What church do you go to?' He in fact was an atheist, an active member of the Communist Party and a street corner orator in promotion of his creed. As politely as he could, therefore, he told the old lady that he did not believe in Christianity and had no time for church. She was rather taken aback but before he left she pressed upon him a copy of William Barclay's Daily Study Bible Commentary: Luke. He accepted it out of politeness, stuck it in his coat pocket and thought no more about it until he came across it again a few weeks later. For some reason he decided to look into it and ended up by reading it completely through, rather like a novel. He read it again, twice, and then said to his wife, 'That's the truth I've been looking for.' It changed his whole life. He joined up with his nearest church and soon was immersed in its work, eventually becoming a Sunday School teacher and much more. When Willie Barclay was told this story years later he simply remarked, with characteristic humility, 'That shows the power of the Word of God.'

Finally, another experience of my own. I lead a group to the Holy Land every year and always take them, as part of the pilgrimage, to visit the Garden Tomb in Jerusalem. One year the man in charge who escorted us round was an Anglican clergyman.

On hearing my Scots accent he enquired as to which part of Scotland I hailed from. When I answered 'Glasgow', he said, 'Do you by any chance know William Barclay?' When I told him that Willie and I were close personal friends, he almost fell down and worshipped me. 'When you return home,' he said, 'please tell him that you met a man who owes far more to his books than any words could express.'

It would be impossible to give an exact tally of all the people who have been helped by William Barclay's writings, but the total number must be enormous and certainly covers the world. It is a well-known fact, too, that many ministers have been glad to make much use of Barclay in the preparation of their sermons. Willie was always delighted about this, taking it as a great compliment and also as an added indication that his books were serving a useful purpose. I recall a radio programme in which he had the question put to him, 'Do you not object to ministers making use of material from your books for their sermons?' 'Of course not,' was his reply. 'That was one of the reasons I wrote them.'

William Barclay the writer was criticised in some quarters—and at times severely—for being 'a *populariser* of the New Testament'. The label was attached to him in scorn but it is really a badge of honour, for he was instrumental in making the New Testament real and relevant, and fascinating at the same time, to a multitude of men and women all over the world. It was said of Jesus that the common people heard him gladly. The reason was that they were able to grasp easily what he was talking about and at the same time they recognised that what he had to say was of immense importance. I do not consider I am being in the least irreverent when I say that William Barclay counted it the highest accolade his books ever could receive that millions of people 'read them gladly'.

I have already drawn attention to the fact that William Barclay often asserted that he was no original thinker and that he regarded himself as no more than a kind of 'theological middleman'. His gift, as he saw it, was not somuch to initiate new thought as to distil the findings and the thoughts of others into a 'plain' language that 'plain' men and women could readily understand. Even if we accept his own assessment here without reservation, it must be said that his ability to perform this kind of distillation and transmission was remarkable to the point of being unique and he employed it with great diligence and unflagging energy in his Master's service, particularly in the exposition of the New Testament.

His major writing, measured not only by its volume but also by its significance and its influence, most would readily agree, was his Daily Study Bible series, covering all the New Testament books. This 17-volume series has, at the time of writing, sold more than 3 000 000 copies in the English language edition. Although not his first books to be published, the Daily Study Bible volumes were what first brought him the world-wide acclaim which is still accorded to Barclay the writer.

This fact gives the story behind the Daily Study Bible series an additional flavour. It is a somewhat romantic and whimsical tale, especially as Willie himself used to tell it. The Church of Scotland's

Publications Committee, whose Publishing Manager was Revd Andrew McCosh, a long-standing personal friend and former fellow student of William Barclay's, had been rather tentatively experimenting with the idea of commentaries on selected books of the Bible. One or two had already appeared when suddenly Willie Barclay had a call from Andrew McCosh. 'We've been rather let down in our planning,' said McCosh. 'Could you help us out, Willie, and do a commentary in a hurry on one of the books of the Bible? That will fill the gap and give us time to look around for someone really good.'

It was in response to that *cri de coeur* that Barclay wrote—indeed in great haste—his Daily Study Commentary on the Acts of the Apostles. It was an immediate and tremendous success and soon he was invited to follow it up. In the end what was originally intended as a 'one-off' contribution became that complete series of 17 volumes covering every New Testament book which has sold so many copies and aided so many people. Some would call it luck, Willie would have said it was God.

The Daily Study Bible provided an example of how William Barclay's major concern and chief motive in his writing were always the communication of the Good News contained in the New Testament. In conjunction with The Saint Andrew Press he originated what was called the Goodwill Scheme in relation to the Daily Study Bible. By virtue of this scheme all the volumes of the series were made available to missionaries and other church workers overseas at a price which was only a very little over production cost. On these books Willie took no royalty. In addition, he and The Saint Andrew Press agreed to a number of indigenous language editions without any royalties and without any translation fees.

All of the many Barclay books found a public and most of them sold very well—for religious books one might reasonably say 'phenomenally well'. I have served for many years as industrial chaplain to the Glasgow end of Collins Publishers. Some considerable time ago the then manager of Fontana department invited me into his office and confessed he had a problem. 'I've been given copy for a book of prayers by William Barclay and I've been instructed from "on high" to print 25 000. It must be madness to bring out such a large edition of a book of prayers. Do you think I ought to raise the matter with the Board and ask them to think again?'

I hastened to assure him that in my opinion, with William Barclay's popularity and with what I knew of the superb quality of his prayers, 25 000 was not a great risk. He was still a bit dubious, but went ahead with the first print of 25 000. It was sold out in a very short time and many reprints have had to be made. Many other books followed, as the appendix shows.

Apart from his books, William Barclay over the years had a massive published output in terms of magazine articles. For many years, for instance, he wrote a weekly article for *The British Weekly* and also wrote an article for every edition of *The Expository Times*. How he managed to fit these into his enormously busy schedule, without, I think, ever missing a deadline, is amazing.

There is another aspect of Barclay the writer

which I have chosen to include in this chapter, partly because it is difficult to include anywhere else but also because it has a right to feature here even though it does not embrace any published work. I am referring now to the colossal number of letters which he wrote over the years. These were a ministry in themselves.

William Barclay in the years I knew him was a very punctilious correspondent. After he became well known, and particularly once had had commanded a widespread and enthusiastic following through his broadcasting, he was the regular recipient of a massive postbag. Every day many people wrote to him, often to say a thank you for some helpful word heard or read, but often also seeking advice in regard to some personal problem or trouble. He acknowledged every such letter and never failed to respond to a plea for counsel.

In physical terms this amounted to a substantial undertaking, but he never grudged or resented the time it occupied. He looked on it always as part of his ministry. He must have written thousands of letters of this sort over the years and some of them, I know, developed into a long-running correspondence. He took pains with them and was never content just to rattle them off in slap-dash fashion in order to get a chore out of the way. Every letter mattered to him for the simple reason that every correspondent mattered and his letters, even when short, were models of graciousness and kindliness. Many people from all walks of life still treasure the letters that William Barclay wrote to them.

Two things particularly marked his letters, as indeed they marked all his writing: his regard for words and his regard for people. He always seemed to choose the right word for the occasion and for the individual. The person to whom he happened to be writing was the person who mattered most to William Barclay at that precise moment.

This was so whatever the social position of the person to whom he was writing, and whatever the age. Here is an example, a letter written in his Renfrew days to a ten-year-old, and lovingly and gratefully preserved in the years since.

My dear John,
This is just a short note to congratulate you on doing so well at school. I was very proud indeed to see one of our boys walking up to get so high a prize. Keep it up and you will do great things. I don't need to tell you to work hard because I know that you do. Well done indeed and may you have many more successes.
With every good wish,
Ever yours,
William Barclay.

Let me give you another example by a somewhat older 'fan' of William Barclay's and written at a much later period. The supplier of the letter writes: 'I was getting over a heart attack and feeling rather low and dispirited and then I heard one of his lectures on television. I was much uplifted by it and by the conviction with which he spoke. I felt I just had to write and tell him how much it had helped me. The result was the letter I enclose. He had taken the time and trouble to write to me while he was on holiday. When he died I felt, though I had never met him, that I had lost a real friend.'

William Barclay's letter reads:

My dear Friend,

Your very kind letter reached me here at Inverness where we are spending a few days' holiday. I am very glad indeed to know that the television discussion helped and comforted you, and I am most grateful to you for writing to tell me so. I can assure you that your letter is a great encouragement to me.

I hope that you will soon make a good recovery from your heart attack.

With all thanks,

And with every good wish

And every blessing,

Yours sincerely,

William Barclay.

Most of the many letters he wrote were of that kind of length and on that kind of level, although a goodly number were longer and plumbed deeper depths. All of them, whether short or long, bore that same stamp of concern for his fellow-men, for the Saviour's sake, which characterised all his books.

6: THE BROADCASTER

It was his books that made him universally known. It is his books that continue in vast numbers to carry his teaching to a world-wide public. His most enduring and most widely spread claim to fame always did and always will reside in them.

But his most spectacular, and in some degree most exciting, acclaim came in the realm of broadcasting. This was certainly much more limited in geographical scope than that provided by his books, being confined largely to the United Kingdom so far as radio was concerned and to Scotland in the field of television. But his success and appeal as a broadcaster were immediate, phenomenal and enduring.

Many factors contributed to the enormous popularity William Barclay achieved as a religious broadcaster, first on radio and then on television. Every one of the qualities which made him so successful in his speaking and in his writing played its part, but there were other elements in his success which emerged only in the heat of the battle.

He brought to his broadcasting that same thoroughness of preparation which characterised all his public speaking. He never allowed himself to go on the air without being completely ready. This was undoubtedly part of the explanation of the colossal impact his broadcasts made. It was, however, only part of it; there were other things, too.

First, and perhaps foremost, there was the man himself. His remarkable personality transmitted itself across the air waves in quite astonishing fashion. There was, too, his photographic memory. He used to say that this was simply one of the gifts with which God had endowed him. He was insistent that he could take no personal credit for the possession of this gift, but must see to it that he employed it to the best possible advantage in the service of Jesus Christ and for the welfare of his fellow-men. Added to this was his keen intellect backed up by a brilliant academic career at school and university.

One of the many outstanding characteristics of Barclay, the broadcaster, was his remarkable time-watching and time-keeping ability. If he was scheduled to speak for 'x' number of minutes, he could be depended upon to speak for precisely that time, no more, no less. This ability was, of course, an absolute godsend, so far as radio and television programme-making were concerned.

He used to tell me that his mastery of the watch in his broadcasting was the direct result of the first broadcast he ever made. It was a 'live' radio broadcast of a Sunday morning church service that was to occupy 35 minutes. William Barclay prepared everything very carefully—just as he was to do many, many times in later years—and, with stopwatch in hand, paid particular attention to the timing.

He worked hard at it and had no doubt, he told me, that the service would last exactly the time specified. When the broadcast took place everything went beautifully according to plan for the first five minutes or so. Then the producer, Reverend Stanley Pritchard, dashed in excitedly to the church from the adjacent control room to announce that owing to a transmission fault none of the service so far had been going out on the air at all. As a result, they would now have to start all over again from the beginning. The trouble was that, since it was a live broadcast and since the following programme could not be delayed, William Barclay, without notice and without time for previous thought, had now on his very first broadcast somehow to compress his carefully prepared 35 minutes into 28. He did it.

It was this experience, traumatic though it was, that liberated him for ever after from any fear or anxiety about time-keeping in a broadcast. On that first occasion an unwelcome accident compelled him to dispense with the typed pages in front of him which he had so carefully prepared and so painstakingly rehearsed. It was about the last situation he would have chosen for himself but once it arose, then, as he put it to me, he just had to get on with it as best he could. His best turned out to be marvellous. He was so steeped in his material that the laying aside of the manuscript became in the event not so much a handicap as an advantage. He said the bulk of what he had intended to say, said it in a completely relaxed and unruffled manner, and arrived at the benediction, without any apparent haste or improvisation, at precisely the second it was due.

This experience set the pattern for the large volume of broadcasting he was to get through in subsequent years. He always prepared assiduously, always wrote out his script in full, always learned it thoroughly; and always delivered the material with that combination of freedom and discipline that was his own special brand. I was frequently privileged to be present at his broadcasting sessions, sometimes live, sometimes pre-recorded. His invariable practice was to deliver verbatim the opening and closing paragraphs of his prepared script, exactly word for word as they had been written. Every word in these sections had been very carefully chosen and it was important that they should all be given as intended, without change or deviation. The rest of what he said, however, while adhering closely in substance to the script, could and often did vary quite markedly from it in detail.

On several occasions he recorded a series of what turned out to be extremely popular television programmes for BBC Scotland on his home ground, Trinity College, Glasgow. These programmes consisted of William Barclay talking for nearly 35 minutes to a studio audience on a New Testament theme; the practice was to record two of the programmes each evening, with a coffee break between and reassembling the audience in different seats. It was a heavy night's work for Willie and I recall one such evening when the workload turned out to be even heavier than usual.

After the first of the two scheduled programmes had been completed, the statutory play-back test revealed that a fault had developed in the recording equipment and that the programme recording had been ruined. Once the mechanical fault had been put right, there was nothing else for it but that the audience should reassemble as it had been and that Professor Barclay should go through the whole lecture again from beginning to end.

What I personally found most remarkable that night was not only the manner in which he accepted this added burden as 'just one of those things' but also the manner in which he delivered his lecture the second time through. It was just as fluent and just as relaxed and just as fascinating as the first effort; but what struck me most about it was the fact that there were considerable verbal differences between 'take one' and 'take two'. In the second run, the opening and closing sections were exactly as before, the typed script lying on the desk before him being again reproduced word for word, but between these two sections much was different, both in regard to the things he said and in regard to the order in which he said them. Yet once again, as in the first run through so in the second, the timing was precisely as desired, to the very second. That, I think, illustrated for me, more than anything else, what a master he was of his broadcasting craft.

That was not my first acquaintance with this particular facet of William Barclay's genius. Years earlier he had asked me for the use of my church for a radio broadcast he was to make. It was to be a live transmission of a church service of a 'popular' character. Willie, being at the time a lecturer at Trinity College, did not have a church of his own and I was pleased to make mine available to him for the broadcast.

He chose not to conduct the service from the pulpit but had a table and microphone set up in the chancel. I occupied the pulpit, from where I conducted some preliminary devotions for my own people who were, of course, to form the congregation for the broadcast. Just before we were due to go on the air, Willie handed me some papers and said, 'Here's a copy of my script. You'd better have it so that, if anything goes wrong with me during the broadcast, you'll be able to carry on with the service.'

At that time I had never done any broadcasting and you may readily imagine, I am sure, the state of near paralysis created in me by this sudden statement uttered in such matter-of-fact tones. But I recount this tale not to draw attention to the reaction it produced in me, but because of the way it illuminates two very pronounced Barclay characteristics.

The first is the one I have already been discussing, his meticulous preparation which permitted him in his broadcasting to combine a relaxed freedom of delivery with an exhaustive treatment of his subject and always to do so with exactly the timing that the producer desired.

I sat in the pulpit that day with a copy of his script on my knee while William Barclay presented his 35-minute popular church service. He started off word for word as the script had it, but then came a period of puzzled concern for me, when I wondered if he had lost his place in the script. I began to hear paragraphs spoken in a different order from what lay in front of me. I began to hear the thoughts set out before me being spoken in words that were different from those that I was reading in the prepared text. After the initial panic subsided, I realised that what he was doing was giving, with little reference to the script, a very free but at the same time remarkably accurate version of what he had written. Then, just about two minutes before the end of his address, he settled once more into an exact reproduction of the text that was there before us both.

It was in this somewhat dramatic fashion that I first encountered the Barclay style of broadcasting, which I was later to hear and see so often on radio and television.

That day also illustrated another notable Barclay characteristic. When he pushed those papers into my hands and said, 'You'd better have them so that if anything happens to me during the broadcast, you can carry on'; he was not trying to be over dramatic and certainly not facetious. He really meant what he was saying. For him the thing that always mattered most was that the Lord's work should go on. Nothing was more important than the communication of the Gospel; so it was that, if disaster or death were to strike in the middle of a broadcast, his main concern was that the Lord's word should still be proclaimed.

His broadcasting popularity was phenomenal; initially in the field of radio, where his unmistakable gravelly voice became a beloved institution, as he spoke to all and sundry about the things of Christ and his Gospel in terms that everyone could understand. As in his writing, so in all his public speaking (and private conversations, too, for that matter) he had no time for language that cloaked the meaning. Words, he passionately believed, were intended for the conveying of their user's thoughts in a way that could be readily grasped and understood. Nowhere was this maxim of his put into practice with more striking success than in his broadcasting. The extremely large audiences that were attracted and held by his radio broadcasts were drawn from all walks of life; and very many of these listeners were greatly helped, often finding the key to renewed life, by what they heard him say so plainly concerning Jesus Christ and his Gospel.

When he finally entered the field of television broadcasting his audiences grew in number but continued to be drawn from all areas of society. His popularity and his influence increased too; yet he very nearly never appeared on television at all.

He liked radio broadcasting and felt completely at home before a microphone, whether it was in a studio or in a church or indeed anywhere. But for years he refused all invitations to appear on television and determinedly resisted all attempts to persuade him otherwise. He was convinced that he was not suited to this medium and that he would not be effective in it.

I like to think that I had something to do with his finally being persuaded to 'give it a go'. He used to say I had. But it was, I think, his wife who did the trick in the end and finally induced him to yield to the years of cajoling by Ronnie Falconer, BBC's Head of Religious Broadcasting in Scotland, backed up by the persistent pleadings of friends such as myself.

What a blessing it was that he was eventually persuaded to change his mind about appearing on television. He was a marvellous success from the outset; despite the fact that many of the pundits agreed with his own assessment that he was entirely the wrong formula for success on the small screen. Apart from his rasping voice and his broad Scottish accent, his style of presentation was what nearly all the experts reckoned a sure recipe for failure.

The setting of his television programmes was invariably a lecture room with an invited audience gathered before him in serried rows; he simply lectured in much the same fasion as he did to his students. Using the rostrum as his base, his lecture notes carefully laid out on the lectern, he strode up and down the platform, speaking as he went, with an occasional glance at his typewritten script and the words pouring forth in an unbroken torrent all the while.

This kind of presentation was considered to be the kiss of death for any kind of programme but especially for one of a religious nature. The disadvantages, moreover, were compounded by the fact that Barclay made things very difficult for the cameramen by virtue of his incessant movement; aggravated by his habit of frequently fingering his hearing aid (without which he was totally deaf). The recipe seemed all wrong; yet it produced a delicious dish.

One series succeeded another, for a number of years, and the Barclay programmes gathered an immense following. They were transmitted on Sunday evenings and they were the chief talking point in many places all over Scotland on the following Monday mornings. What was perhaps most impressive and certainly what was most pleasing to Willie Barclay was that a vast proportion of his regular viewers came from the ranks of those who attended church hardly ever or not at all.

I remember well one particular Monday morning during one of these series. For many years I had been joining in once a week for their morning training session with the players of our home-town football club, Motherwell. It so happened that I was in the dressing room on the Monday morning in question. One of the first-team professionals, not a churchgoer, called across to me as we were changing, 'I was watching your friend last night. He was marvellous. He's the best thing on television—I never miss him.'

There is no doubt that many thousands found great enjoyment in viewing Barclay's television programmes and a great many of these derived much help from them for the business of living out life day by day. If, then, the ingredients were so wrong, and the experts seemed to agree that they were, how was it that the final product was so universally acceptable? The answer to that question is undoubtedly to be found in other ingredients in the mixture which some of the prognosticators failed to take sufficiently into account.

These other ingredients included things to which I have already drawn attention, like William Barclay's unique ability to speak to anyone and to everyone in immediately intelligible language, coupled with his large reservoir of background knowledge and his readiness to spare no pains in his preparation. The chief ingredient of success, however, was without any doubt the man himself. Charisma is always difficult to define and it is never possible to describe it precisely or fully. But certain qualities undoubtedly contributed to William Barclay's.

First, his humanity; he had a broad and deep concern for his fellows. This meant that he was often an 'easy touch' for someone with a hard luck story. At times he could seem very naïve in this regard, but he was prepared to be exploited a score of times rather than risk turning his back on a single opportunity of extending help where it was genuinely needed. This kind of compassionate outlook towards others came through loud and clear in his utterances.

Another important factor was that he was very down to earth. He was just as much at home chatting with the car-park attendant as holding conversation with the Queen or some civic or ecclesiastical dignitary. I recall going with him to see our beloved Motherwell play on a very wet and windy winter afternoon. It would clearly have been much more comfortable to sit in the grandstand and, left to myself, I must confess that is where I would have gone. Willie, however, wanted 'to be with the people' and so we stood on the terracing with the majority, getting soaked through just as they were, but enjoying at the same time the warm-hearted camaraderie of the crowd.

William Barclay was fond of quoting Abraham Lincoln's saying that 'God must have loved the ordinary people very much for he made so many of them.' William Barclay loved them too, and that was part of the reason that he could and did speak to them with such clarity and establish such a warm and enduring rapport with them.

This brings me to his humbleness of spirit; and this too was surely not only part of his personal charm, but also a contributory element in his prodigious success as a communicator. He was, and remained, a very humble man even when he rose to the dizzy heights of fame and popularity. He never lost sight of the fact that he too was a mortal man with human faults and failings. In consequence he never grew conceited or vainglorious about his talents and achievements but maintained sincerely that any skills he might possess were the gift of God and that, therefore, any success he might achieve was God's doing. Because of this he was able to put himself in the other person's place and never patronised any individual or audience he was addressing.

One mark of his humbleness was his enjoyment of stories against himself and he loved to retell them. Here is one he greatly liked. It was immediately following one of his television series. A lady approached him in a hotel lounge and proceeded to congratulate him enthusiastically on the programme. In the course of a short ensuing conversation she said, 'Tell me, Dr Barclay, where is your church?' To which he replied, being at the time Professor of Divinity and Biblical Criticism at Glasgow University, 'Oh, I don't have a church at the moment.' 'Never mind,' the lady said, laying her hand comfortingly on his shoulder, 'I'm sure you'll get one soon.'

I can still see his shoulders heaving and his eyes twinkling as he told that story. He thoroughly enjoyed it, just as he enjoyed telling about the time he pulled in to a garage for petrol during the time when another series of his was showing on television. The petrol pump attendant kept staring at him and Willie thought to himself that here was another 'fan' summoning up the courage to speak. At last the attendant spoke up, 'I've seen you on television haven't I?' The Professor nodded assent, 'Yes, probably.' 'I knew it, I knew it!' cried the attendant triumphantly. 'You're one of those telly comedians, aren't you?'

Many factors contributed to his quite phenomenal popularity as a broadcaster and many more stories could be told. It seems to me more fitting, however, to close this chapter with an example of the very real help his broadcasts gave to very many men and women. I quote from a letter recently received.

> I was a young housewife with three small children and that particular day I was really down. I'd been to church in the morning, particularly needing something to help but I got nothing from the service and God seemed very far away. Late that afternoon Willie Barclay spoke on the wireless and it was as if he spoke only to me. Before he finished, I was filled with peace and found myself able to pour out my heart in prayer. Things have never looked so black again.

7: THE PEOPLE'S MAN

One facet of William Barclay's character which has already been underlined was that he was very much interested in people, but this was so big an element in his make-up that it deserves a further and fuller mention. He liked people and liked them for themselves and not for any position they might hold. Barclay was an enthusiast for the works of Robert Burns and was in total agreement with the bard's great poem about the intrinsic value of the individual.

> The rank is but the guinea's stamp,
> The man's the gowd for a' that!

As has been said before, William Barclay was fond of company and got on well with people. Despite being at heart a rather shy person, which may surprise many, he was a very good mixer. He was once the weekend guest of the Queen at her Scottish home, Balmoral Castle, and I know that he greatly enjoyed the experience; but he enjoyed equally well meeting and conversing with people of humbler origins and position.

When he went to Collins Publishers, after his university retirement, I used regularly to have lunch with him in the course of my weekly visits to the firm as industrial chaplain. We usually went to the workers' self-service canteen and Willie used to enjoy sharing a table with some of the men and women from the factory floor.

One day we were in the company of two girls in

their late teens. After a little general conversation, one of the girls said to Willie, 'I've seen you on the TV.' He acknowledged this with a smile and a nod of the head and the girl continued, 'You're not bad.' Willie treasured that remark ever after.

His affinity with 'ordinary' people, his liking for them and his often instantaneous rapport with them, was characteristic of the humble man he was. He was never a very practical man, rather 'handless', as the Scots idiom might express it, but he was never unwilling to take off his jacket or dirty his hands if he felt he could be of any assistance to someone in a spot of difficulty.

Witness the following anecdote (and I quote from a letter received in 1983).

> I had bought during the winter of 1958 an old 1951 Morris Minor 'banger', my first car. It behaved reasonably well until one Sunday it refused to start. I had just come out of Dennistoun Baptist Church where William Barclay had been the visiting preacher. With my heart and mind still mulling over the brilliant points of the sermon, it took me a few minutes to realise that the 'banger' was being truculent.
>
> Soon the place was deserted, or so I thought, until from behind the car I heard the booming voice of Willie Barclay, 'Get in, laddie, put her into second and I'll give you a push.' I protested that I would leave the car and return later to attend to it, but he insisted, 'Get in, laddie. I'm sure she'll start with a good push.'
>
> He was right. We had hardly travelled ten yards down Meadowpark Street when the car coughed into life—and a quick glance in the mirror revealed that great man rubbing both hands together, a broad smile creasing his face as he observed the result of his efforts. Such was the man.

Many people could, and frequently do, recount similar true tales of William Barclay. He was always eager to get alongside people where they were. He liked them and enjoyed being with them. That is why he was so often found playing football with the Sunday School children at their annual summer trip or in the middle of a group of Youth Fellowship members at the tea-break during their conference, or going out of his way to show friendship.

A well-known (now retired) Scottish Sheriff told me this story. William Barclay was a life-long enthusiast for the Boys' Brigade and helped the movement in many ways, not least by the writing of several of the handbooks which the BB produced annually as a guide for the Sunday morning Bible Class, central to the organisation and its aim of the 'advancement of Christ's Kingdom among boys'. He also occasionally attended the BB Council Meetings to give Bible talks to the Council members.

Let the Sheriff take up his story. 'There was one occasion when we were in Birmingham, and, being the only Scot on the Committee, apart from the Chairman, it became my duty to look after William Barclay. There was a civic reception, and suddenly I realised that he was not there. Panic stations—with his deafness in a strange city. When we got back to our hotel, there was the bold Dr Barclay sitting writing at a desk, quite unconcerned. On being asked where he had got to, he replied that several members of his Renfrew congregation had been moved to Birmingham and he "just couldn't be in Birmingham and not call on them." While we had been enjoying the festivities of the civic reception he had quietly visited something like fourteen homes in the city. How typical of him.'

One of the best of the many stories that will illustrate how William Barclay was so much a man of the people is this. He was heading one night for a destination out of the city to be the guest speaker at a formal dinner. Driving along wearing his dinner suit, he suddenly realised he was completely out of cigarettes and in the days before he gave up smoking that was a circumstance not to be relished. But it was well into the evening and the shops were shut. The only places still open where cigarettes might be obtained were the public houses. Not to be deterred, evening dress notwithstanding, the bold Willie drew up at the next pub and went inside to purchase cigarettes. The appearance of this resplendently-attired figure caused an immediate hush in the busy bar, then recognition dawned—it was during his television days—and the Professor found himself surrounded by enthusiastic devotees of his programmes, anxious to express thanks and eager to ask questions. There was an animated session of religious discussion in that public house bar, with William Barclay at the centre. It could have gone on all night if Willie had not had to drag himself away because of his dinner speaking engagement. When he left it was to a chorus of cheers and, what's more, as he himself used to describe it, 'they wouldn't even let me pay for my cigarettes.'

Indeed, he was a man of the people and this was in no small measure due to the fact that he was also a man of God. These two facets of William Barclay— man of the people and man of God—were never opposed but always complementary. Any danger there might ever have been of his trying to be a man of the people at the expense of being a man of God may well have been averted by a simple incident in his early ministry which had a salutary effect upon him.

He had taken his car to the garage for a minor repair and he waited around (in his clerical collar) while a young mechanic struggled with the job. Suddenly a spanner slipped, causing the lad to graze his knuckles, and the pain brought from his lips a violent oath. The youth was instantly embarrassed at swearing in front of the minister and apologised. Not wishing to appear stuffy, Willie B murmured that he didn't mind, to which the lad replied with considerable feeling, 'Well, you bloody well should.'

He was a man of catholic and often what might be termed plebeian tastes. He had a number of hobbies, none of them exotic but each belonging to a field with which many ordinary people were able to identify. He was a keen philatelist and had gathered together over the years a considerable stamp collection. He was a student of steam loco-motives and, while I am not aware of his ever writing a book on this subject, (although it would not greatly surprise me to discover that he had done so), he had a number of books dealing with it in his own library and at times was prevailed on to speak about it.

Music was another of his loves and, while he was not averse to the classics, the Gilbert and Sullivan operas were his passion, especially when it was a D'Oyley Carte performance. He used to mark the D'Oyley Carte Glasgow dates well ahead in his diary and tried hard (not always successfully, it must be said) to keep them free from any other engagement.

It was his love of music (and partly also his love of fun and his love of Trinity College traditions) that led him to resurrect the Trinity College Choir and give service for so many years as its conductor. It must be confessed (and the erstwhile choristers would, I think, be the first to agree) that he was no great musician really. But he had an infectious enthusiasm for the subject and for the task it imposed on him. Even the choir practices, every Friday afternoon in the first and second terms, were in consequence full of fun and fellowship; and the choir members loved him. A further consequence of their affection was that, when the concerts came along and Willie got up on the podium and began to wave his arms around in time to the music (more or less), they sang for him, always with matching enthusiasm, always with life and feeling, and sometimes quite musically as well. The Trinity College Choir practices and concerts were great fun and William Barclay loved them.

Another element of Barclay, the man of the people, was his love of conversation. He liked few things better than an animated conversation with a friend or a group of friends; unless it were a debate with such a group, and even better if there was some controversy within the group. He was an excellent conversationalist himself and brilliant in discussion, although frequently frustrating to the point of exasperation. This was because he enjoyed an argument for argument's sake and as a result it was not uncommon to find him changing horses in midstream. I have heard him more than once make a positive statement towards the end of an argument that was practically in direct contradiction of a statement he had made equally positively at the argument's beginning. He was in fact an incorrigible 'coat-trailer', and was very fond of stirring up a good argument. All of this tied in closely with the fact that he maintained active membership of several clubs whose meetings centred round theological discussion.

William Barclay was also a man of the people in his passion for sport. Ball games were a love of his life, particularly golf, cricket and, most of all, association football. As has been indicated, he was a good sportsman himself in his younger days, displaying considerable skill on the athletics track, the golf course and the football field. As time went by and physical participation had, of necessity, to be relinquished, his interest as a spectator and follower did not wane. Even when, in his latter years, his emphysema and associated ailments kept him indoors most weekends and he was no longer able to go and see his beloved Motherwell play their matches, he used to keep in close touch with their performances by dint of comprehensive eyewitness accounts from me and/or his son Ronnie as well as by devouring the newspaper reports. As a result, although he had not attended a football match for a number of years prior to his death, he remained very much *au fait* with the football world and its events. That was why, for instance, invited at short notice to take part in a BBC sports programme one evening, he was able to appear before the cameras wearing a Motherwell FC tie (which he had borrowed from me an hour or two earlier) and speak with perfect aplomb and quite knowledge-able authority about the Scottish football scene.

In earlier years he rarely missed attending a foot-ball match when it was on offer, especially if Motherwell or Scotland were involved. A contem-porary of Ronnie Barclay's recalls being at the manse in Renfrew one Saturday afternoon for Ronnie's birthday party and how they were all des-patched at 2.30 pm to Love Street football ground to watch St Mirren play Glasgow Rangers, return-ing to the manse after the match to resume the festivities.

He disliked being deprived of a football match unnecessarily, but always had his priorities right. The then Secretary of the Glasgow Provincial Sun-day School Union, James Greig, told how the year that William Barclay was President he, Greig, inad-vertently called a committee meeting for the same night as a Scottish football international match. He had a visit the following morning from President Barclay to reprove him for his error, but Barclay nevertheless was in the chair at the meeting, though it is likely that some of his heart was at Hampden Park.

Another feature of William Barclay, man of the people, that many people found endearing, was his lively and often irrepressible sense of humour. This in earlier days sometimes found expression in prac-tical jokes. One who as a 16-year-old attended a conference at St Andrews for Sunday School teach-ers in 1940 has this recollection of the event more than 40 years later. William Barclay was the chief speaker but was the leading light in other ways too.

'He encouraged a few of us one night to tie together, with rope, door handles of various bedrooms. He gave us his alarm to waken us at two o'clock in the morning and we got up and tied the doors as advised. The task was just completed when the air raid sirens wailed, whereupon we had to undo the work at record speed. We naturally were not very popular, except with Willie. I also remember how on the train journey home he flew paper gliders up and down the corridor of the train. He had a very joyous spirit.'

This joyous spirit frequently found expression in his speech, both public and private, which was marked by a lively wit and a fund of stories. He was not one who disapproved of humour in the pulpit and often used it to help get his message across, like in his children's address on the theme of 'counting your blessings'. 'If you have a sore neck,' he said, 'thank God you're not a giraffe—whatever your circumstances there's always something to thank God for.'

His platform speeches were liberally adorned with witticisms and funny stories and so were his private conversations. He had a natural and spontaneous sense of humour. This is aptly illustrated by the following (apocryphal?) Barclay story. He was conveying some members of his Trinity College Choir to a concert when one of his rear seat passengers sang out, 'Didn't you see that old woman you nearly knocked down?' 'Never mind,' replied Willie, 'I'll get her on the way back.'

And how could anyone who had ever seen it forget the sight of Willie Barclay enjoying a good joke, whether told by himself or someone else, shoulders heaving, eyes sparkling, face alight?

It seems not inappropriate here to make reference again to William Barclay's essential and unchanging humbleness of spirit. For this in no small measure not only enabled him to get alongside the people with whom he was seeking to communicate but also endeared him to them.

His humility was perhaps never better illustrated, certainly never more dramatically, than by the fact that he once declined the invitation to be Moderator of the General Assembly of the Church of Scotland. In those days the committee which decided upon the next Moderator or, at least, decided upon the nominee to be presented to the Assembly, which is virtually the same thing, did so without the prior knowledge or consent of the nominee. The first the chosen man knew about it was usually when he received a telephone call from the secretary or the convener of the committee to say that he had been selected.

It caused great consternation when Willie B, on receiving such a call, replied that he was touched by the honour done him but that he must decline. A plea that he should reconsider his decision made no difference to the outcome. Willie steadfastly refused to accept what many count as the highest accolade the Church of Scotland can bestow. Who else could or would have said 'no' to such an opportunity?

A great many people were surprised and many, many more were sorely disappointed at his decision, for he would have been a very popular choice. But his refusal was a mark of the man and of his humility in particular. He simply did not reckon that he was cut out for that sort of task.

'It's just not my scene,' I remember his saying to

me. 'I think I will be making more valuable use of the time it would occupy by using it to do the things I have some ability to do, teaching and writing.'

Incidentally, William Barclay's refusal of the moderatorial nomination, and the disappointment (and embarrassment) occasioned by that refusal, led to a change in the nomination procedure. Ever since that time it has been required that anyone proposed for office as Moderator must have given prior consent.

How much the Church would have enjoyed seeing him in the Moderator's Chair was perhaps further evidenced by the tremendous reception given William Barclay by the General Assembly of 1974. He was retiring from his professorial Chair at the end of the summer and was called to the General Assembly in May of that year in order that the Moderator might, in the name of the Church, express thanks to him for all that he had done for Christ and his kingdom, his kirk and its people.

After the Moderator had paid his tribute and William Barclay had replied in typical fashion, there followed perhaps the most enthusiastic and most sustained standing ovation the General Assembly has ever witnessed. I know that Willie himself was deeply moved, as were most of us who were privileged to be present.

8: THE MAN OF CHRIST

The heart and the secret of William Barclay's prowess and success were his devotion to Jesus Christ. From an early age he was Christ's man through and through. The difference his Christian faith made to him was perhaps never better shown than when he sustained the tragic loss of his daughter Barbara to which I shall make reference later. It was shown also in his attitude to his deafness.

William Barclay became almost totally deaf at an early age and from then on he was able to hear nothing at all except with the assistance of his hearing aid. Many would have found an affliction like this intolerable. Barclay, however, simply accepted it and got on with his work. More than that, he saw the advantages in his unwanted adversity and exploited them to the full. He used to maintain that sleep was for him much more refreshing than for most other people because, once his hearing aid was laid aside, he was assured of sleep that was undisturbed by any extraneous noise.

He used to say, too, somewhat mischievously no doubt, that when someone's talk or conversation was dull and boring he could find refuge in his deafness simply by switching off his hearing aid. It certainly is the case that he frequently switched it off when he was working at his typewriter. The absence of any sound whatever in his ears, he claimed, greatly aided his concentration. This was an example of his belief in Paul's dictum that all things work together for good for those who love God.

It was not inappropriate that much of Barclay's earlier writing was done on behalf of the Boys' Brigade. The motto of the movement, 'Sure and Stedfast', could well have been his own. His allegiance to Jesus Christ was the dominating feature of his life and his many talents were all harnessed to the task of advancing Christ's kingdom not only among boys but among all mankind. Concern for the spread of the Gospel was what made him decide for the ministry in the first place. God's call came to him in the form of a challenge to devote his talents to that cause—and that same concern was behind all that he did from then on.

When he became a very successful writer of religious books (and many of his writings reached the best-seller category), the Barclay books began to bring him in a great deal of money. The financial side of the matter, however, was never of major significance to him. He never argued about royalty arrangements or contracts to my knowledge; in fact I never knew him to discuss this aspect to any great extent. His habit was simply to accept whatever contract his publisher drew up for him and to sign it in the invariable assumption that what was being contracted to him was fair and reasonable. He was not much interested in the money that his books were earning for him. From his first book to his last the purpose that constantly motivated his writings was that of communicating something of the Gospel of his Lord and Saviour, Jesus Christ.

At the same time, although never anything else but Christ's man first and foremost, Barclay was always his own man so far as the understanding and interpreting of the faith was concerned. This meant that he did not always follow what was considered to be the orthodox line—not always, although more often than some people might care to admit.

As has been noted, William Barclay liked nothing better than to 'stir things up' in a theological discussion and he frequently did this very thing, usually tongue in cheek. This was a characteristic that led, rather unfortunately, to his having attributed to him a number of so-called heresies that did not in fact represent the views he held. He was, as a matter of fact, much more conservative on many subjects than is sometimes imagined.

At the same time his was not always what might be termed a routine orthodoxy: and this on occasion earned him severe disfavour from those who thought such an orthodoxy was the only kind that was approved by God. On one particular occasion this led to his receiving a very cruel blow which wounded him sorely. He was giving a radio series of short morning talks on the miracles of Jesus. One morning he was speaking about the stilling of the storm. In the course of his talk he said that he could not tell what exactly took place on the Sea of Galilee on that long ago occasion but he did know for sure that Jesus had stilled the storm of fear that was raging in the hearts of the disciples. He went on to say that the most important thing this story had to tell us today was not what physical events occurred on Lake Galilee 19 centuries ago, but that we could be confident that Jesus was able to still any storm in our hearts today. He said, too, how thankful he was that he had found this proved true in his own experience. When his daughter had been drowned, Jesus had stilled the storm of grief and sorrow in his heart and given him the strength and courage to go on.

A few days later, pain etched on his face, he showed me a letter he had just received. The writer upbraided him for what he alleged was a heretical treatment of the miracle and continued, 'I am now able to see why God killed your daughter. It was lest you should corrupt her any more with your heresy.' The letter was signed 'Yours in Christ'.

I was shocked and angry. Willie was also shocked as well as being deeply hurt but what he said was, 'Whoever wrote that deserves our pity rather than our anger.' Christ's man that he was, the graciousness of his Lord was showing through in him.

Another instance of this Christ-given graciousness of which I had personal experience occurred the night that William Barclay, along with Professor James Stewart of Edinburgh, was being honoured by *The Upper Room* magazine with the award of a citation for outstanding contribution to the cause of Christ and his Gospel. The award ceremony took place in the Assembly Rooms in Edinburgh before a large gathering.

Pastor Jack Glass, a Glasgow Protestant zealot, chose to picket the Assembly Rooms in company with a number of his followers in order to demonstrate their antipathy to William Barclay and what they regarded as his heretical teaching. As the guests converged on the Assembly Rooms, they were there with placards and banners carrying messages such as 'Barclay is a heretic' and 'Barclay is an enemy of the Gospel'. I was so indignant at the demonstration that I said to the bearer of the 'Barclay is an enemy of the Gospel' banner, 'That's quite ridiculous. William Barclay has done more to commend the Gospel in our generation than any other individual.'

Willie's own reaction was typically different. When he came along, saw the demonstration and read the slogans, he went across to Pastor Glass himself and with hand outstretched, said, 'Let's shake hands, Jack. Despite our differences of opinion, we are both on the Lord's side.' I thought then, and I think still, that that was a very gracious action indeed. Jack Glass, I am sorry to say, refused the offered hand.

William Barclay was often very unfairly accused of heresy or apostasy. I recall being the guest speaker at a conference of Christian women not long ago. They were Americans, mostly the wives of US servicemen stationed in England. I made some remark about William Barclay in the course of one of my addresses. Later on, one of the delegates drew me aside and said to me, 'Wasn't it a great pity that Dr Barclay gave up the Christian faith before he died?' That was, of course, utter nonsense and quite ridiculous: and I told her so. I went on to ask, 'How did you happen to have such a strange and so false idea?' 'I think I read it somewhere,' she replied, 'in some magazine or other.'

I thank God that most Americans have a more accurate picture of William Barclay, the man of Christ. I quote, as two random examples, from letters I received from the USA. The first came from a Baptist layman in Richmond, Virginia.

> Dr Barclay, in my estimation, was a wonderful person, one who helped me immensely on my Christian pilgrimage, especially through his writings. . . . I purchased

the first volume of Matthew and then procured all 17 volumes. Since that time I have procured most of Dr Barclay's books.

In 1975 my wife and I visited the British Isles and went to Edinburgh for three days. While there I called Dr Barclay in Glasgow and arranged to visit him the next day. I met him at Collins Publishers and we had about one and a half hours together.... Upon my return to America I wrote thanking him for taking the time to talk with me. This resulted in a continuous correspondence until two weeks before his death when I received my last letter from him.

Dr Barclay had already endeared himself to me through his writings, but he meant much more after having met and corresponded with him. He was a godly man and one that I shall always be proud to acknowledge as friend and as benefactor.

The other came from Arizona and here is part of it. 'I'm a 59-year-old retired firefighter who recently converted from the Catholic faith to the United Presbyterian Church. I am also a new student of the Bible. Fortunately I discovered and started using Dr William Barclay's books, the Daily Study Bible series, as an aid to understanding the Bible, and his books have really been an inspiration to me; a person so very anxious to know and understand God's Word.'

On more than one occasion I have heard it alleged that William Barclay did not believe in the life to come. People have pointed to some parts of his writings, such as in *Testament of Faith* or *Arguing about Christianity*, and asserted that they have found in his own words an admission that he did not believe in the life everlasting. I can only plead that they read his words with greater care. Willie never at any time said that he did not believe in the life everlasting. What he did say, and more than once, was that Christ was so good a Master and Friend that even if there were no life to come, he (Willie Barclay) would still consider him worth following. Even if it were proved that there is no heaven, the Christian faith would still be worth embracing and would still get his vote.

That is a quite different thing from saying that he did not believe in the life to come. Indeed, he did believe in that life to come, and continued to do so to the end.

His belief in the life everlasting was never more real and never more evident than when his daughter, Barbara, was drowned at the age of 19. It was the very same year that Willie received his Doctor of Divinity degree from the University of Edinburgh. All his friends rejoiced with him in this honour and there were, as a result, a number of associated celebrations. One of these was in Trinity College where Barclay students past and present gathered to do honour to the new Doctor. I was privileged, by Willie's own invitation, to be present at this very happy event and when it was over I drove Barbara to the railway station. She had plans different from the rest of the family for the evening and I took her to get her train. I had known her well for a long time, not only meeting her in the Barclay home but also frequently at Fir Park, for she too was an ardent Motherwell supporter.

That was the last time I ever saw her. Later that summer she was on holiday with her fiancé in Northern Ireland and one day disaster overtook them in the middle of a yachting expedition in Lough Foyle. No one ever ascertained exactly what had occurred but their sailing dinghy was found empty with no immediate trace of its occupants. The boy's body was fairly soon retrieved but agonising weeks were to pass before Barbara's body was found. I thought much then, and I have thought much since, of one of those odd and some-times very moving coincidences with which life is besprinkled. In his speech of response at that Trinity College celebration from which I drove Barbara to her train, one of the pleasantries with which Willie made us laugh was this. Whenever he was away from home lecturing or preaching, as he often was, it was one of his inflexible rules that he telephoned home to his wife every night and she, consequently, never needed to telephone him. The news of the offer of a DD came to his home during one of these absences and Kate, understandably, rushed at once to the telephone to let him know. 'When I was told my wife was on the phone,' he said, 'I was sure it could be nothing but news of a catastrophe. And so, for me, DD will always be associated with Death and Disaster.' And two months later Barbara was dead.

It was a dreadful calamity, the worst by far that had ever befallen the Barclays. And they all felt it very keenly. The wound went deep and the scar never went away. It so happened that, during the winter following, Willie was to be the guest speaker at our annual Sunday School Parents' Night in High Carntyne Church. The circumstances being as they were, I suggested that I make other arrangements, but he would have none of this. In the course of his address there came one of the most heart-stopping moments I have ever known. He began to make an allusion to Barbara and just could not get the tense right. 'My daughter is—was—is—was. . . .' He was clearly in the grip of great emotion as he, the supreme master of words, struggled to find the right words now. I thought he was going to break down completely, but he recovered himself and continued his address. He did not refer to the incident, nor did I, but it demonstrated all too plainly how much he had been wounded by Barbara's loss.

If ever any personal catastrophe was of a magnitude to be termed a test of faith, this was surely it. William Barclay's faith was adequate to the need even of this heart-rending hour. The very week after Barbara's death he was in the pulpit of Palmerston Place Church in Edinburgh, proclaiming the Good News of a loving God whose grace freely offered through Jesus Christ was enough to see men and women through any and every need.

It was then I heard him affirm quietly but firmly his own confident belief in the life everlasting. He derived great strength and comfort from that assurance. His picture of the 'better land' might well differ at times from what some reckoned to be the orthodox conception but he was in no doubt that that future better land was a reality.

He had this faith when Barbara was drowned and he had it still at his own ending.

It is true that he had a number of theological convictions that many found disagreeable. It is true that he was time and again a non-conformist in matters of doctrine and of ecclesiastical opinion. But he was never the non-scriptural heretic that some would have liked to make him out to be. An honest reading of his Daily Study Bible volumes is enough to prove otherwise.

In any event, whatever heresies a man is supposed to entertain ought always to be considered and judged in the light of the kind of Christian he is; and Willie Barclay was beyond dispute a real man of Christ. Under the auspices of Glasgow University's Extra-Mural Education Department, he led for many years a highly successful and extremely popular Biblical Studies Class in Motherwell. I had the privilege of taking it over from him when his doctor advised him to do less. For quite a time after my succession the class continued to be known as 'Dr Barclay's Class', and the members were grateful for the way in which I made a point of bringing to them occasional messages from Willie and of keeping them up to date with his health and his activities. I well remember (will I ever forget?) one faithful member remarking one night, apropos of one of 'The Doc's' more controversial statements, 'Dr Barclay is too nice a man to believe all the things he says.'

Christ's man he was, through and through, and Christ's man he remained to the end. It so happened that I was alone with him for half an hour or so just two hours before he died in Mearnskirk Hospital on the outskirts of Glasgow. As I sat with him, just the two of us, it was plain that he had not long to go; and I thought to myself, 'We'll miss you, Willie, we'll miss you very much. But as for you, you've booked your ticket to heaven.' Was I being ridiculously sentimental? Was I being stupidly naïve? Perhaps. But that is how I felt then, and I think that it is how I feel still.

9: JOURNEY'S END

When William Barclay retired from his Professor's Chair in October 1974, a few of his friends, myself included, had the idea of organising a thanksgiving event in tribute to all his magnificent work, particularly as a communicator of the Gospel of Jesus Christ. This was to be an occasion of rejoicing and of gratitude for all he had done for, and been to, so many people through his lecturing, his speaking, his preaching, his writing and his broadcasting.

In due course the arrangements were made and a public gathering was held on 8 November 1974, in Wellington Church, Glasgow, a large church in whose parish the university buildings stand. After a great deal of thought, we called it 'The Plain Man's Tribute to William Barclay' and a general invitation was extended to any who wished to attend.

I had the honour of being the Chairman of this tribute meeting. It was a glorious and fitting occasion. We were anxious to reflect the different aspects of Barclay the man and the servant of Christ, particularly as a communicator of the Gospel; and we attempted to do so by having a number of different people speak briefly about one feature or another of the man and his work. I hope it may help to highlight some facets of the picture I have been trying to paint here of William Barclay if I quote a little of what took place on an evening the memory of which he prized until the day he died.

In introducing the proceedings I explained that we had planned this public tribute as a kind of 'everyman's' thank you to Professor Barclay and so the speakers had been carefully chosen to represent the masses of people from all walks of life who were, as I put it, 'debtors in the faith' to him.

After the opening praise and a prayer of thanksgiving led by Revd Andrew Herron, Clerk to the Presbytery of Glasgow, we called on Revd Bob Brown, one of Willie's former students, who was then in his first ministerial charge. He thanked the Professor not only for what he had taught his students but even more for the interest he had shown in them as individuals and for his willingness to give of his time and his wisdom so generously in order to help and advise whenever help and advice were sought.

'We knew that you were already very busy and were probably in fact engaged at any given time in writing three books, two lectures and a speech; but you always gave us your undivided attention with no hint of hurrying us, as if the only thing that mattered at that moment was what we might say to you. I and all your former students thank you tonight because you communicated the Gospel to us, not only by what you said, but even more by what you were. We loved you for it then and we love you for it now.'

Bobby Watson, who was then the Captain of Motherwell Football Club First XI, took the rostrum next, to say that his tribute represented the gratitude of the players and the spectators of the sporting world of Scotland. Some of them, he said, were committed Christians like himself, many were not church attenders at all; but the majority were devoted 'fans' of the Barclay television programmes and many owed a great deal to the Barclay writings.

The next speaker was from William Barclay's youth group at Trinity Church, Renfrew, many years previously. Archie Maynard was now holding down a responsible job in the shipyards and now also an elder in that same kirk. He spoke with feeling and enthusiasm of the tremendous impact that Barclay had made upon the young people of the church and of the whole town at that time. Many, including himself, had had their lives profoundly influenced and even dramatically changed through this man.

Ian Chapman, of Collins Publishers, long a personal friend of Willie's, spoke of the enormous and astounding popularity and world-wide influence of his ministry in print—through his books, so many in number and published by so many different publishers; and through his magazine articles, weekly, monthly and occasional, so numerous that no man could possibly number them.

Ronald Falconer, then the Head of Religious Broadcasting in Scotland, paid tribute to his phenomenal success and acclaim as a broadcaster both on radio and on television. The most remarkable feature of it all, he said, and one which spoke volumes for his unique gift of communication in this medium, was the manner in which television crews were captivated by him. Television crews were notoriously hard-headed and blasé, but when Barclay was 'performing' they actually listened with rapt attention.

Since William Barclay was always very interested in the 'plain man' and we had deliberately styled the evening as 'The Plain Man's Tribute', we selected at random an elder from a Glasgow church to speak on behalf of all the many 'ordinary' Glaswegians who adored him. The lot fell on David Wylie and he stated with great simplicity that thousands of people like himself with no academic training or background blessed the name of William Barclay for all that he had taught them of the New Testament and its message.

We did not confine the list of speakers to the UK because, of course, our guest of honour's fame and influence had extended far beyond these shores. Revd Bob Martin from Princeton, New Jersey, flew across the Atlantic specially to speak on behalf of the scores of thousands in USA, who were Barclay admirers and beneficiaries. One of his many apt remarks was this: 'William Barclay has the mind of the scholar and the heart of the artisan and early in his ministry he discovered the wisdom of being simple without being simplistic.'

Revd Colin Campbell, William Barclay's own parish minister and a close personal friend of many years' standing, spoke of Willie as a family man, and paid tribute not only to the guest of honour but also to his wife Katherine who had done so much to help keep her husband's feet always firmly planted on the ground.

Revd Stanley Munro, a lifelong friend of Willie's and a former fellow student, spoke of their college days together and of how all Willie's contemporaries knew, even then, that he was destined for great things. Stanley it was who handed over the cheque which represented the donations that had flowed in from all over the world to mark the gratitude of many thousands, a cheque which the recipient used to found 'The Barclay Lectureship in Communication of the Christian Gospel'.

Another feature of the evening which spelled out its own tribute in unmistakable fashion was the re-assembling of a number of former members of Trinity College Choir. Once again, under the baton of their professor-conductor, some forty ministers expressed not only their faith but also their gratitude in song.

The climax of the evening was reached with William Barclay's reply. It was vintage Barclay; humble and grateful, brilliant and moving. In typical fashion he had us one moment rocking with laughter and the next deeply moved, at times almost having the feeling that in a second or two we would actually be seeing the New Jerusalem before our eyes. The main theme of his speech was thankfulness: to his parents; to his schooling; to his students; to his friends; to his wife and family; and especially 'to God who has been so astonishingly good to me all the days of my life.'

It was the same feeling of thankfulness, I fancy, that prompted him to donate the cheque he received that night to the funding and the founding of a lectureship in communication of the Christian Gospel. We who were the sponsors of the night of tribute and the accompanying fund certainly thought nothing could have been a more fitting use of the monies contributed. We became the Trustees of the Lectureship, with myself as Chairman, and in due course arrangements were made for the first series of lectures, with Willie himself a very interested party to our deliberations. Bishop David

Sheppard of Liverpool, former England test cricketer, agreed to be the first lecturer and this delighted William Barclay immensely.

Unfortunately and sadly, Willie did not live to see or hear the first lectures, much as he had been looking forward to doing so. In consequence, what were originated as lectures in honour of a living great, became lectures in loving and honoured memory of him. So far the lectures have taken place every second year. David Sheppard duly delivered his in October 1978. Professor Robin Barbour was the lecturer in 1980 and Gerald Priestland in 1982. At the time of writing, the 1984 lectures are in sight and The Rt Hon Lord Tonypandy (George Thomas), former Speaker of the House of Commons, has accepted our invitation to give these. All of these lecturers have proved themselves in the realm of verbal communication and so fit in well to a pattern that is intended both to honour a supreme communicator and also to advance the promotion of the Christian Gospel to which he had devoted his life.

William Barclay retired from his professorial Chair in his 67th year. He could have continued until he was 70 but he chose to go then. His reasons were two-fold. For one thing he felt strongly that older men should not hold on to their offices and their jobs too long. So he said on that night of tribute in Wellington Church, 'It is much better to retire a year too early than a year too late.' For another thing he was attracted by the thought of how much more writing he could get done once he no longer had to devote time to preparing and delivering university lectures. He was particularly captivated by the prospect of writing for Collins a series of commentaries on the books of the Old Testament and so to continue and complete the work he had already done for The Saint Andrew Press in writing his 17 volumes of Daily Study Bible commentaries covering the whole of the New Testament.

Sadly, things did not work out quite as had been hoped. Collins did in fact fix him up with an office and secretary in their Glasgow premises. This was an arrangement very pleasing to Willie and his time as a 'Collinsian' was a very happy one for him. But the prodigious writing output of earlier years was not nearly matched in the years of retirement from which he and so many others had hoped and expected so much; the retirement years were to be heartbreakingly few. In particular, apart from an unfinished manuscript on the Psalms, his great ambition to write a complete Old Testament commentary did not get off the ground.

This is not to say that these were fruitless years. For most other men the harvest of these post-retirement years would have seemed rich and abundant. He did some radio, he did some television and he wrote some books. By Barclay standards, however, the output was comparatively small.

The sad fact was that fairly soon after his retirement he began to show unmistakable signs of slowing up. His brain remained as sharp as ever, his knowledge as extensive, his ability to communicate as uniquely effective; but he was not able to concentrate as once he had nor to work so quickly as before or for such long hours. Increasingly often I used to call in to his office and find him asleep at his desk.

The emphysema which had plagued him for years began to take an increasingly heavy toll; and perhaps the extremely heavy workload he had imposed on himself for many years was also now having its effect on his physical resources.

He would not have wished to change the latter, of course, and who could have wanted it otherwise? Because of his chosen way of life he had, I believe, accomplished more than ten other men put together might have accomplished for Christ and his kingdom. Even travelling at the reduced engine-power which was his in these last years, he managed to make magnificent witness for the Gospel not only in speech and in writing but in his person. His mere presence in the Collins building made a considerable impact and his open friendliness and easy approachability, whether encountered in the corridor or in the workers' canteen, endeared him to all.

So far as writing is concerned, one of the most striking things he did in this period was the text he wrote for *Jesus of Nazareth*, the Collins book version of the Zeffirelli film. The book contains superb plates from the film and Barclay's text makes a magnificent accompaniment to them. He wrote a few other things including a series of articles on the New Testament writers. This was done for the Church of Scotland's magazine *Life and Work* and later they were issued as a book.

These 'other things' were now, however, taking a great deal more of his time than they would once have occupied and it soon became evident that the Old Testament series was becoming more and more unlikely. He made a beginning with the

Psalms but did not manage to complete it. The unfinished manuscript was a rather poignant mixture of vintage Barclay and material of much inferior quality. After his death I did my best to separate the nuggets from the dross and so, thankfully, it was possible for a further and final Barclay book to be published posthumously. Collins gave it the title *The Lord is my Shepherd* and, although Psalm 23 is not one of those dealt with in the book, it seemed a most appropriate title to bestow upon the last book from William Barclay's pen.

Willie was very keen to keep working to the very end of his life; this he did. Even in his last days in hospital he had books at his side for review. It was a great sorrow to all his friends that the end was not so far distant as we had all hoped and expected it would be on that tribute night. In my Chairman's remarks that evening I had said, 'We are assembled here not to bury William Barclay but to praise him; not to bury him indeed, for this retired university professor is already well and happily begun on a new literary life. God grant it may be long as well as successful.'

In the event it was quite short, little more than three years; and he was only a year or so into his retirement before his remarkable powers showed signs of waning. Nevertheless, a fair amount of quality Barclay emerged even in this closing chapter. His writing I have already mentioned. As for television, although he made no more series, he did make a few striking television appearances. His radio broadcasts were not so frequent either, but what there were were as full of popular appeal and as effective as ever. But he scarcely ever preached, and his public speaking occasions became fewer and fewer. Nevertheless they were sufficient to show that he could still gather an audience of any description into the hollow of his hand by the sheer magnetism of his personality. I remember, for instance, that he was included on the speech list at the annual Collins dinner in Glasgow. Here was a hard-bitten assembly of some 400 executives, foremen, printers and salesmen. William Barclay 'wowed' every one of them and also gave them a Gospel message to think about, if they cared to do so.

In a way I probably grew even closer to him during those last years. We used to lunch together once a week when we would discuss everything and anything. I missed him terribly when he died and I miss him terribly still. But he went from the world as he always hoped he would go—quickly, once his writing days were over.

Work was his consuming passion. Ever since he had decided to be a minister, he had worked with unsurpassed industry, first to learn his trade and then to practise it. He was never happier than when he was engaged, in some way or other, in the task of communicating the Gospel of his Saviour and Master. It was fitting then, although it carried inevitable sadness for his family and friends, that he should have little time to spend in idleness.

He came to his 70th birthday on 5 December 1977 and on the same day he left his Collins office for the last time. For the previous two years his health had been noticeably deteriorating. The week following his birthday he became much worse. Very soon he was admitted to hospital and in January he died.

It so happened that I called in to see him just before the end. I had not known that the end was so imminent and it was with some sense of shock that I heard the ward sister tell me there was really no point in going to his room. The family had been sent for and he was quite unconscious. However, she was kind enough to allow me to be with him for a while and for a time I sat at the bedside of my beloved friend knowing that I would never look on his face again in this life. I felt sad, but I knew that the sadness was selfish, mourning for myself and my own loss; and I forced myself to think rather of all the glad thankfulness I should feel for all that I and the rest of the world owed to this man for whom the sands of time were fast running out.

This note of joyful gratitude was the one that was dominant in his funeral service, despite the sorrow that was also inevitably present. Even the weather put on mourning garb that day. It was a bleak Scottish winter's day with snow lying on the ground and sleet slanting incessantly down from a lowering sky. The fact that the whole world seemed to be in mourning for William Barclay was typified for me by the fact that I noticed a policewoman, directing the funeral traffic, quietly weeping as she went about her task.

It was, of course, with heaviness of heart that we gathered, hundreds of us, into the church standing in the crematorium grounds for the service that was to be conducted by Willie's own minister and personal friend of many years, Colin Campbell. But the atmosphere of the service was mainly one of triumph. This was absolutely right and exactly as William Barclay would have wanted it, given that there had to be a funeral service. He used often to declare in his gruff, authoritative tones that he would prefer that there was no funeral service for him when he died. This was one of many topics of friendly argument between us. I used to try to repel this suggestion with as much force as I could muster; but he would persist with the unyielding obstinacy he so often summoned to his side when in his heart of hearts he knew that he was continuing to argue mainly for the sake of argument.

'Funeral services,' he would say, 'are an unnecessary fuss and an unnecessary cause of additional grief. They are superfluous so far as Christians are concerned, for the Christian knows better than anyone else that the body has done its work and is no longer of any importance. It should just be disposed of as quietly as possible—the real person no longer has any part of it. In any case,' he would go on, 'funerals are often an occasion for fulsome and insincere tributes being paid to the departed; and I do not want flowery and flattering eulogies spoken of me when I depart.'

I used to try to point out to him that this was a selfish attitude. Of course the Christian knows that his body is of no consequence after death; but surely, I said, you must allow your many friends the opportunity to pay their respects to you, as they will certainly want to do.

In the event, the funeral service was the kind of simple and sincere occasion of which he would, I am sure, have approved. We sang a Scottish metrical psalm and we sang one of his most favourite hymns, 'My times are in thy hand'. It was fitting that we should sing this hymn at his funeral service.

He particularly liked the words of the third verse:

> My times are in thy hand:
> Why should I doubt or fear?
> My Father's hand will never cause
> His child a needless tear.

and, to those of us who gathered in that church for William Barclay's funeral, the last verse seemed particularly appropriate:

> My times are in thy hand:
> I'll always trust in thee;
> And, after death, at thy right hand
> I shall for ever be.

It was appropriate because William Barclay had often sung these words himself and they joyfully expressed his steadfast faith in the life to come.

The minister read some of the triumphant Scriptures that proclaim so gloriously the Christian assurance of the life everlasting; and he led us in a magnificently moving prayer of thanksgiving for the life and work of William Barclay. That prayer I felt was just right for the occasion and just right for William Barclay's memory. I feel sure it was a prayer that William Barclay would have been humbly pleased to acknowledge; yet the odd thing is that it was not at all a prayer he could or would have written himself.

William Barclay never used the traditional 'thee' and 'thou' when addressing the Almighty in prayer. For all the time I had known him he had firmly believed in setting aside that kind of language in public worship as being a hindrance rather than a help in the endeavour to lead men and women into the presence of God. Colin Campbell's prayer was couched in the more traditional style of 'thee' and 'thou' still favoured by many Scottish ministers.

Although William Barclay felt strongly that it was a mistake to continue to frame public prayer in these terms, he would have been pleased and touched by this particular prayer. It was so patently sincere and it gathered up tenderly and sympathetically all the thoughts and feelings of the congregation meeting together that day to take sad but grateful farewell of a man loved so much.

Colin Campbell and William Barclay had been friends for many years, even before the crosscurrents of life decreed that Colin should become Willie's minister; and the fact that Colin persisted with prayer language such as Willie himself would never use did not diminish that friendship in the slightest. This was just another measure of the true Christian character of William Barclay. He did not fall out with any man or take offence at him because he disagreed with him about this or about that.

It is a sad fact that it did not always work like that the other way round. William Barclay was subjected to many an unkindness and to many a hurt simply because someone disagreed with him in his understanding of some aspect of the faith they held in common. Many a time, for instance, he has shown me a letter—perhaps following a broadcast—which attacked him quite viciously for some supposed heresy or the like; and in all probability the letter would be signed 'Yours in the Master's service', or in similar fashion.

William Barclay, for his part, returned good for evil when anyone attacked him for his views; and consistently replied to unfair criticism or even abuse with graciousness and charity.

I want to put on record again, before I bring these

very personal reflections on William Barclay to a close, that his belief in the life everlasting was real and strong. I was both surprised and shocked to read in one of the newspaper obituaries of him that 'William Barclay had severe doubts about the life hereafter.'

That was simply not true. He had serious and penetrating doubts about the ideas some people held about the nature of the life of heaven; but he had no doubts whatsoever that beyond this life Jesus had in store for his people something even better and richer. I often heard him affirm strongly and unambiguously his belief in the life to come, and you will find the same affirmation many times in his writings.

I remember particularly his saying to me, after Barbara's death, that he had never been more sure of the life to come than then; and he never wavered from that firm conviction.

That is why I do not think of William Barclay as merely dead. I miss him still, but, like the millions of others who have cause to give thanks for him, whether or not they ever knew him personally, I rejoice that he is now more gloriously alive than ever before.

William Barclay was a big man in every way. He was glad to be alive and he enjoyed life immensely, finding its gladness and its satisfaction all the deeper because he knew Jesus as his Saviour and Lord.

We may rejoice that he is still vibrantly alive. Earth became much the poorer for his passing but heaven was made that much richer. His influence upon the world and its people still goes on and will do so, I believe, as long as time endures.

APPENDIX:
THE BARCLAY BOOKS

William Barclay was himself never quite sure how many books he had had published; and even now it is virtually impossible to give an exact number. The difficulty is not simply that he wrote so many books, but that a number of his writings have appeared in print in different forms, either in whole or in part. It can be said, however, that at this time of writing there are 68 of his books in print in the UK and the USA. A complete list of these books now follows with the name of the publisher and also a brief indication of the theme, except where the title itself gives sufficient indication of that. UK titles available in USA are marked with an asterisk and the US publishers' name is given in brackets.

THE SAINT ANDREW PRESS

*The Daily Study Bible (Westminster Press) is an exposition of the entire New Testament in a series of 17 volumes and already some 3 000 000 copies have been sold of the English language edition. William Barclay treats each New Testament book in a similar fashion and sets out the text in a form that lends itself to 'daily study'. He begins by giving a general introduction to the book in question, explaining its origin and its situation, both historically and theologically. Then he works through the entire book, splitting it up into small daily sections, making his own translation of the Greek text before expounding it. In doing so he lights up the text vividly with his explanations of its background and original meaning, illuminating it still further with a wealth of appropriate anecdotes told in his characteristically racy style.

★Ambassador for Christ (Judson Press) A revised edition of one of his earliest books, this is an exciting account of the life and teaching of the Apostle Paul.

★And He Had Compassion (Judson Press) is a treatment of the miracles of Jesus that emphasises he is still able to accomplish wonderful things in human lives today.

★And Jesus Said (Westminster Press) Most of the parables of Jesus are explained and expounded in this volume. Barclay's masterly talent for filling in the religious, historical and geographical background brings the stories alive and at the same time makes their message plain and relevant for today.

★The Old Law and the New Law (Westminster Press) is an examination of the present-day relevance of the Ten Commandments along with a consideration of the continuing relevance of the Sermon on the Mount.

★The All-Sufficient Christ (Westminster Press) The sub-title is 'Studies in Paul's Letter to the Colossians'.

Flesh and Spirit is an examination of Galatians 5:19–23, carried through by making an intensive study of the Greek words used.

Arguing about Christianity is the transcript of the tapes of seven informal conversations on religious topics between William Barclay and Iain Reid.

Communicating the Gospel The first three chapters were originally the Laird Lectures and the expansion gives a treatment of the whole question of understanding God's Good News, tracing back to the Prophets, and of making it known.

God's Young Church is a description, based on the Book of Acts, of the characteristics of the early Church.

The Making of the Bible tells how the various books that now comprise the Bible came to be classed as Holy Scripture.

*The Men, the Meaning, the Message of the Books (Westminster Press) is a look at the authors, the various themes and the unifying central message of the New Testament books.

Turning to God Here Barclay examines in some depth the meaning of conversion with special reference to the Book of Acts and the linguistic (Greek) background.

The King and the Kingdom has as its subject the Old Testament vision of the Kingdom of God and the way it is all fulfilled in the Kingship of Jesus.

COLLINS

The Plain Man's Book of Prayers; More Prayers for the Plain Man; Prayers for Young People; More Prayers for Young People; Prayers for Help and Healing
In a series of 'Plain Man' books William Barclay takes the designated theme and works through it simply but profoundly in language that is for the most part non-academic and always free from theological jargon and religious gobbledygook. The above are collections of prayers, each accompanied by an appropriate Bible reading, that cover a multitude of daily life situations and are couched in typical Barclay language—direct, simple and arresting.

The Plain Man Looks at the Beatitudes; The Plain Man Looks at the Lord's Prayer; The Plain Man Looks at the Apostles' Creed

Jesus of Nazareth is Barclay text accompanying still pictures taken from a television life of Jesus.

The Mind of St Paul is an outline of the thinking of the Apostle as revealed in his New Testament letters.

Ethics in a Permissive Society is the version he prepared for book publication of what were originally the Baird Lectures.

The Plain Man's Guide to Ethics is a follow-on.

*The Lord is my Shepherd (Westminster Press) is an exposition of five of the Psalms put together after his death (by James Martin) from material he left unfinished.
*In the Hands of God (Westminster Press) is a collection of journalistic-type Barclay writings of a devotional and reflective nature.

SCM PRESS

The Mind of Jesus deals with Jesus' early ministry.
Crucified and Crowned deals with the events of our Lord's Passion and Resurrection and the beginnings of the Christian Church.
Epilogues and Prayers is a book of devotions for use by groups as well as by individuals.
Prayers for the Christian Year
The Gospels and Acts is a consideration of the background, origin, authorship and general content of these books.
Jesus as they saw Him examines the various titles ascribed to Jesus by his contemporaries as recorded in the New Testament.
Many Witnesses, One Lord
The Master's Men is a book about the Apostles.
A New People's Life of Jesus
New Testament Words is an exposition of a number of New Testament Greek words.

OTHER UK PUBLISHERS

Great Themes of the New Testament (T & T Clark)
Introducing the Bible (International Bible Reading Association)
A Life of Christ (Darton, Longman & Todd) In this

Barclay wrote the text for a strip cartoon presentation of the Gospel Story.

The Character of God (National Christian Education Council)

ONLY IN USA

Westminster Press
Fishers of Men has to do with Christian preaching and teaching.
Introduction to the First Three Gospels
Introduction to John and the Acts of the Apostles
The Lord's Supper
Letters to the Seven Churches gives an exposition of the appropriate section in the Book of Revelation.
Men and Affairs is a collection of Barclay pieces written originally for *The Expository Times*.
The New Testament: A New Translation is William Barclay's own translation from the Greek, lovingly prepared—in his own estimation his *magnum opus*—and is separate from the translations he made for his Daily Study Bible volumes.
The Promise of the Spirit is a consideration of the biblical teaching about the Holy Spirit.
Testament of Faith is his own 'spiritual autobiography'.

Judson Press
By What Authority is a treatment of the authority of Jesus, the Old Testament and the Church.

Word Inc
The Lord's Prayer

OTHER BARCLAY BOOKS (no longer in print)

In an endeavour to make this list of William Barclay's

books complete, I add now in chronological order a note of all other publications I can trace, with a statement of the publishers and date of publication. Some of these books, as the titles themselves may suggest, were used, in whole or in part, as the basis of a later Barclay volume.

New Testament Studies (Scottish Sunday School Union, 1937)—his first ever published work.

God's Plan for Man (The Boys' Brigade, 1950)

One Lord, One Faith, One Life (The Boys' Brigade, 1952)

God's Law, God's Sovereignty, and God's Man (The Boys' Brigade, 1954)

God's Man, God's Church and God's Law (The Boys' Brigade)

God's Law, God's Servants, and God's Man (The Boys' Brigade)

Camp Prayers and Services (The Boys' Brigade)

New Testament Wordbook (SCM, 1955)

More New Testament Words (SCM, 1958)

Educational Ideals in the Ancient World (Collins, 1959)

The Way, the Truth and the Life (Collins, 1960)

The Christian Way (Collins, 1962)

Christian Discipline in Society Today (Fellowship of Reconciliation, 1963)

A New Testament Wordbook (SCM, 1964)

The Epistle to the Hebrews (Bible Guide Series, 1965)

The First Three Gospels (SCM, 1966)

Seen in the Passing (Collins, 1966)

The Bible and History (Butterworth, 1968)

Introducing the Bible (Denholm House Press, 1972)

The Gospels and Acts (SCM, 1972)

Jesus Christ for Today (Collins, 1974)